DISCRIMINATION

JAPANESE AMERICANS
STRUGGLE FOR
EQUALITY

DISCRIMINATION

JAPANESE AMERICANS STRUGGLE FOR EQUALITY

by
LIANE HIRABAYASHI

Rourke Corporation, Inc.
Vero Beach, Florida 32964

Cover design: David Hundley

∞ The paper used in this book conforms to the American
National Standard for Permanence of Paper for Printed
Library Materials, Z39.48-1984.

Library of Congress Cataloging-in-Publication Data
Hirabayashi, Liane, 1965-
    Japanese Americans struggle for equality / by Liane
Hirabayashi.
        p.   cm. — (Discrimination)
    Includes bibliographical references and index.
    Summary: Identifies discrimination and discusses how
Japanese Americans have struggled for their civil rights.
    ISBN 0-86593-183-6 (alk. paper)
    1. Japanese Americans — Civil rights — Juvenile litera-
ture.   2. Race discrimination — United States — Juvenile
literature.   [1. Japanese Americans — Civil rights.   2.
Ethnic relations.]   I. Title.   II. Series.
E184.J3H53   1992   92-14633
305.895′6073 — dc20   CIP
                                          AC

PRINTED IN THE UNITED STATES OF AMERICA

CONTENTS

DISCRIMINATION

JAPANESE AMERICANS STRUGGLE FOR EQUALITY

1 What Is Discrimination?

Discrimination is a complex, dynamic process that sometimes occurs when two apparently different groups interact. A person is a member of a group as a result of his nonmembership in another group of the same kind. For example, a French citizen will consider herself to be in a separate group from a citizen of Belgium. Group membership may be determined by such characteristics as nationality, age, gender, level of education, political beliefs, language, or religion. In the example of the French and Belgian citizens, if both are members of the Socialist Party, then they belong to the same group, in contrast to members of the Communist Party. A group classified by racial, national, tribal, religious, linguistic, or cultural background is known as an ethnic group. As a nation of immigrants who have come from all over the world, the United States is a society made up of people from many different ethnic groups, such as Jewish Americans, Irish Americans, and Chinese Americans.

Nonmembership in a group is based on the consensus by the group's members about what characteristics are not appropriate. These characteristics are arbitrary, in that their importance in determining membership varies from society to society. For example, among Arabs, language and social habits are important characteristics in differentiating among themselves. In South Africa, skin color, or race, is the major factor in determining social status. The caste system in India divides the society by occupation; a person's membership in one caste is hereditary and cannot be changed.

Discrimination results from the interaction between two groups of unequal power. The more powerful group, which is called the majority group, is determined to maintain the boundaries that distinguish itself from the other group, called the minority group, thereby ensuring the majority's continued superiority. The discriminatory practices used by the majority group to maintain these boundaries range from categorization through stereotypes to extermination. The minority group being targeted by discrimination may react in numerous ways, such as struggle, compliance, or retreat. For example, the minority group, in the face of hostility, may choose to reduce its contacts with the majority group, forming a relatively self-sufficient community within the larger society. Another reaction is to attempt to break down the barriers constructed by the majority group, through civil disobedience and lawsuits.

Prejudice and Discrimination

Prejudice is sometimes believed to be the cause of discrimination. Discrimination is a more complex phenomenon, however. Prejudice is derived from the word "prejudge," which means to form an opinion without a careful examination of the facts or circumstances. A prejudiced person will approach a situation with a predetermined attitude, often negative, and will act based on his prior attitude rather than on the unfolding reality. For example, a person prejudiced against dogs may feel that all dogs are vicious, violent animals that will attack without reason. Such a person will walk across the street to avoid someone walking a dog, even though the dog appears to be acting contrary to the prejudiced opinion. Similarly, an employer who is prejudiced against an ethnic group may refuse to hire an individual who she has classified as a member of that group, no matter how qualified the person.

Japanese American kindergarten students learning about Martin Luther King, Jr.; knowledge of America's multicultural heritage helps to combat prejudice and discrimination. (David Young-Wolff/PhotoEdit)

Prejudices held by individuals are not the real problem; rather, it is the reinforcement of such prejudices within a group that is the cause of discrimination. Discrimination occurs when a group agrees to hold a prejudice against another group and to act on this prejudice to keep itself separate from the other group. Once the group achieves this consensus, they determine ways to reduce interaction between the two groups. In this way, prejudiced attitudes become a part of the majority group's image and become embedded in the social structure.

Stereotypes

The process of discrimination can be considered in terms of stages, beginning with stereotypes. Stereotypes allow members of one group to characterize members of another group in terms of broad generalizations. Because groups will form a distinctive culture, one group will select the obvious traits of another group, exaggerate these traits, and apply them to all the members. These stereotypes are reinforced through use and soon become group definitions, no matter how inaccurate. Moreover, once a person is classified as a member of a certain group, she will be assumed to possess all the traits stereotypically associated with that group.

Often, physical traits are translated into mental traits. For example, one of the stereotypes about Asians in the past was their untrustworthiness. This attribute was derived in part from the appearance of their eyes as slanted, which translated into having a sly, cunning nature. A prejudiced person who classifies someone as an Asian will have no compunction about lying to or cheating the Asian, since any actions by the Asian will be interpreted as motivated by a profoundly deceitful nature. Interpreting an individual's motivations based on stereotypes can be at best bewildering to the individual and may lead to serious misunderstandings.

Although some stereotypes may appear superficially positive or harmless, such as that all African Americans are musical, the use of such stereotypes is negative, because it prevents the ability of individual members of a group to be perceived as unique human beings. Stereotypes are ultimately dehumanizing; they stunt the potential of interactions between group members on a more profound level. Furthermore, stereotypes often initiate more serious types of discrimination, because they allow members of one group to regard the members of another group as less than human. If one believes that Native Americans are dirty savages, then statements such as "The only good Indian is a dead Indian" can be taken seriously and acted upon.

Once stereotypes are established, a majority group will avoid interaction with the minority group, except under very controlled situations in which the minority group is obviously at a disadvantage. If the minority group is perceived as getting too numerous, laws will be passed preventing further immigration. The minority group is also deprived of equal opportunity in housing and employment, and may be denied the right to own land or a business. Immigrant groups may be denied citizenship.

Segregation

If the minority group begins to struggle against these limitations, the majority group may resort to the more drastic measure of segregation. Segregation physically contains a minority group within the society. Strict laws are enacted and enforced regarding the minority group's access to public places, to certain types of employment, and to housing. The minority group is not allowed to interact with the majority group; seemingly trivial things such as public water fountains are segregated. The minority group may accept this status and try to work internally to improve their lives. On the other hand, the group may continue its struggle. Such attempts to overcome segregation are often met by violence, such as the murders of Civil Rights workers in the 1960's.

Once a minority group is segregated, a perceived external or internal threat may trigger the majority group to take more

This Japanese American student is learning Spanish. (Mary Kate Denny/PhotoEdit)

extreme action with relative ease. War and economic depression are examples of external and internal threats. More extreme actions include isolation through apartheid or concentration camps, exclusion through expulsion or exile, and extermination or genocide. The government of South Africa's racist policies toward the non-European population are the origin of the word "apartheid." The deportation of illegal Mexican immigrants to the United States is an example of exclusion through expulsion. The Nazi government of Germany isolated the Jewish people in concentration camps and proceeded to effect the "final solution," genocide.

As a racially and ethnically diverse country, the United States has been the scene of many forms of discrimination, from the massacre of Native Americans to the enslavement of the Africans to the internment of the Japanese. The United States is an ethnically stratified society that is constantly redefining itself, as each ethnic group attempts to overcome the barriers constructed by the majority group, the White Anglo-Saxon Protestants (WASP), to achieve the American dream of equal opportunity.

The predominance of the WASPs in the United States reflects European world dominance at the time that they immigrated to this country. Since their arrival, the WASPs have discriminated against every group they have encountered, beginning with the Native American tribes. Although the Native Americans had numerical superiority, their values allowed them to be manipulated and taken advantage of by the newcomers. In some cases, Native American tribes were completely decimated, by disease and on the battlefield. The remaining tribes were segregated on reservations, land that frequently had little agricultural or economic value.

African Americans also experienced brutal discrimination. The ancestors of most African Americans came to the United States involuntarily, as slaves. Even after the Civil War and emancipation, African Americans continued to be discriminated against openly and violently. Although they have struggled for their civil rights, the social status of this group remains relatively low, and racial prejudice against them continues to provide a formidable barrier to social advancement. The majority of African Americans are segregated in decaying inner cities, where high levels of crime and violence have made it unusually difficult for the new generation to imagine achieving higher social status.

In a stable society, the boundaries erected by the majority group are practically impassable. In a changing society, however, such as in the United States, a minority group may successfully overcome discrimination; the first step is called acculturation, which includes assuming the same values as the majority group. A minority group with similar values appears to be accommodating to the majority. Acculturation leads to more interaction between the two groups and the breakdown of stereotypes. The majority group becomes aware of the more positive aspects of the minority group's culture.

As the minority group becomes more acceptable to the majority, the former is increasingly integrated into the latter. Integration may include the repeal of unfair housing and employment laws, desegregation of schools and other public facilities, and acceptance of the minority group's equal social status.

In the final stage, assimilation, the minority group is absorbed into the majority group. Cultural differences are minimalized or incorporated into the majority tradition. Intermarriage leads eventually to the disappearance of physical differences between the two groups. Few ethnic groups in the United States have reached this final stage. One of the factors in a minority group's ability to assimilate is race. European ethnic groups, such as the Irish and German Americans, have been more successful in overcoming discrimination than Native, African, Hispanic, and Asian Americans. Race is not the only barrier, however. As stated previously, discrimination is a dynamic process; the interaction between the majority and minority groups creates a unique situation, which is affected by many external factors.

2 The Japanese American Experience

The first Japanese immigrants came to the United States more than a century ago, for many of the same reasons as other immigrants: Their homeland was undergoing political and economic upheaval, and many individuals left to seek economic prosperity elsewhere. These immigrants faced great obstacles in their attempts to earn a living and, later, to raise a family.

One hundred years later, the Japanese American community in the 1990's is, in general, a highly successful, fairly assimilated group. Most of the 850,000 people of Japanese ancestry living in the United States are American citizens. About three out of four Japanese Americans live on the West Coast or in Hawaii. The income of the average Japanese American household exceeds the national average. The number of Japanese Americans with a college education is also higher than the national average. The reasons for the success of Japanese Americans lie in their history, which has been marked by extraordinary discrimination and adversity, and in their values, which have been handed down to each generation and have remained fairly constant.

Scholars have noted that a strong sense of ethnic identity persists among Japanese Americans despite the successful participation of many members of their community in

9

mainstream American society. In fact, among Asian ethnic groups, Japanese Americans have the highest outmarrying rate, at 60 percent; in other words, three out of every five Japanese Americans marry non-Japanese. Yet these same Japanese Americans continue to participate in the Japanese community. In their book *Japanese Americans: The Persistence of Community* (1991), authors Stephen Fugita and David O'Brien offer several reasons for "the persistence of community" among Japanese Americans: the strong sense of "peoplehood"; the shared experience of discrimination, particularly the incarceration in concentration camps during World War II; and the extensive network of volunteer associations. Fugita and O'Brien draw parallels between the Jewish American and Japanese American communities. Like the Japanese, the Jews also have been extremely successful in the United States, yet they have maintained their strong sense of community. Because Jews and Japanese were unable to find employment and services in mainstream society, they created communities which were, to a certain extent, self-sufficient. Japantowns, or Nihonmachi, formed wherever there was a large concentration of Japanese. Thus, Japanese were able to run businesses and practice professions within their own community.

The Cherry Blossom festival. (David Young-Wolff/PhotoEdit)

Generations

A unique aspect of the Japanese American community is the distinction between generations. Japanese Americans as a whole refer to themselves as Nikkei. Unlike many other ethnic immigrant groups, the Japanese Americans gave names to each generation: Issei, Nisei, Sansei, and Yonsei, meaning first, second, third, and fourth generation, respectively. Each generation has had very different experiences in the United States. Within the Nisei are a group called the Kibei, who were born in the United States but were sent back to Japan by their parents for much of their education. When they returned to the United States, they were quite different from the American-educated Nisei. One of the reasons that this generational distinction is valid is that Japanese immigration to the United States was restricted to a very short period, from 1885, when Japan lifted its ban on emigration, to 1924, when the United States placed a ban on further Japanese immigration. Although the ban was lifted partially in 1952 and completely in 1965, Japanese immigration after the initial 1885-1924 period was minimal.

Another distinction in the Japanese American community is between the experience in Hawaii versus that on the mainland Pacific Coast states. Hawaiian immigrants were mostly contract laborers who worked on sugar cane plantations. Immigrants to the Pacific Coast had more diversified occupations, working for farmers, railroad companies, and timber mills, for example. In addition, the Japanese in Hawaii did not experience the upheaval of the World War II internment, although they were subject to discrimination and harassment.

Early Immigration: The Issei

The first Japanese immigrants came to the United States in the 1870's. They left a country in great transition. Japan had recently ended more than two hundred years of self-imposed isolation from the rest of the world. This isolation was ended when an American naval officer named Matthew Perry arrived in Edo (later Tokyo) Bay in 1853 to open Japan to the West. He delivered a letter from the President of the United States and demanded that it be given to the emperor. He did not realize that the emperor was merely a figurehead; the country was actually governed by a military ruler known as the Tokugawa shogun. One year later, Perry returned to receive the emperor's reply. The Japanese decided to sign a treaty with the United States in order to avoid the harsh treatment that the Chinese had received at the hands of the British. Japan signed treaties with other Western nations as well in the next few years.

In the next ten to fifteen years, Western nations did not hesitate to use force to remind the Japanese to adhere to the treaties. These incidents led to a political crisis in Japan. In 1868, new leaders took over the government in the name of restoring the emperor. Known as the Meiji Restoration, the movement favored industrialization and Westernization. In order to finance their programs, the new leaders imposed heavy land taxes. They also decreased the price of rice when it rose too high. Hundreds of thousands of farmers lost their land. In 1873, the government enacted the draft to build its military; however, a clause in the draft law allowed students studying abroad and emigrants to be exempt from their military obligation.

The combination of the economic crisis and the draft law made emigration extremely attractive. At that time, the Kingdom of Hawaii was looking for laborers to work on the sugar cane plantations. The native Hawaiian population was severely reduced by disease and felt threatened by the large Chinese population. The Hawaiian government looked to Japan for a new labor pool. Japan was reluctant to send workers overseas for two reasons. First, the government leaders were very sensitive to its image abroad; they wanted other countries to perceive them as a rising world power, not as a source for menial labor. Second, they had already suffered a bad experience in 1868-1869, when several

hundred Japanese emigrated illegally from Japan to Hawaii,
Guam, and California. Those sent to Hawaii complained so
loudly of their treatment that the Japanese government brought
some of them home. As a result, Japan banned emigration. Two
years later, the governments of Japan and Hawaii restored
friendly relations in a treaty. Ten years later, the King of Hawaii
visited Japan to try to convince the government to allow
emigration but was unsuccessful. Representatives of the Hawaiian
government visited Japan in 1882 and 1883 and were still
unsuccessful.

It was not until 1885 that Japan lifted its ban. One of the
people involved in convincing the Japanese government to do so
was an American named Robert Irwin, who had become friends
with the foreign minister of Japan, Inoue Kaoru, and Masuda
Takashi, the president of an import-export company. Irwin was a
representative of the Board of Immigration of Hawaii and also
advised Inoue. Irwin worked out an agreement, known as the
Irwin Convention, between the Japanese and Hawaiian
governments. Under this agreement, which lasted until 1894,
approximately 29,000 Japanese immigrated to Hawaii to work in
the sugar cane plantations. The Japanese immigrants came from
nine prefectures in the southwestern part of Japan: Okayama,
Wakayama, Hiroshima, and Yamaguchi on Honshu Island, and
Fukuoka, Nagasaki, Kumamoto, Saga, and Kagoshima on
Kyushu Island. Irwin, who handled the initial recruitment,
focused on these prefectures at the suggestion of Masuda and
Inoue, who were from Yamaguchi. Masuda helped Irwin by
sending agents from his own company to sign up workers. Irwin
had no trouble persuading Japanese villagers to go, since the
wages in Hawaii were much higher than those in Japan.

In 1894, the emigration was handed over to private companies.
Between 1894 and 1908, approximately 125,000 Japanese
emigrated to Hawaii through these companies. An additional
17,000 went independently. In 1900, the United States
government passed the Organic Law, which made Hawaii a U.S.
territory. As a result, all contracts between the Japanese

companies and Hawaii were declared null and void. The harsh
conditions of the sugar cane plantations made many Japanese
laborers eager to leave. On the West Coast of the United States,
railroad companies, timber mills, and farmers were looking for a
source of cheap labor. The Chinese had been barred from
entering the United States since 1882. Thus, labor recruiters from
the West Coast arrived in Hawaii in 1900 to entice Japanese
laborers to leave the plantations. With the promise of higher
wages and better working conditions, 34,000 Japanese left
Hawaii for California, Oregon, and Washington between 1902
and 1906.

Picture Brides

In 1907, the Japanese government signed the Gentleman's
Agreement with the United States, in which the former agreed to
stop issuing passports to laborers. Japanese immigrants were able
to circumvent this agreement by sending for relatives and wives.
Known as picture brides, these women went through wedding
ceremonies arranged by their parents and the parents of the
absent groom. Having never met their husbands, the women
knew them only by photographs, often liberally touched up to
make the men appear much younger. In 1900, there were only
850 Japanese females compared to 18,000 men in the Pacific
Coast states; of those women, 400 were married. By 1910, the
female Japanese population had increased to 8,000, of which
5,600 were married. By 1920, there were 38,000 Japanese
women on the mainland, of which 22,000 were married. In that
same year in Hawaii, the female Japanese population numbered
48,000. Anti-Japanese groups argued that the emigration of
picture brides was a violation of the Gentleman's Agreement. As
a result of these protests, the Japanese government agreed to stop
issuing passports to picture brides. By 1920, there were almost
30,000 Japanese-American children in the continental United
States. By 1930, there were approximately 68,000 in the
continental U.S. and 91,000 in Hawaii.

Picture brides arriving at Angel Island immigration station, c. 1912. (National Archives/ National Japanese American Historical Society)

The Nisei

Because of the extraordinary discrimination they experienced, many Issei invested all their hopes in their American-born children, the Nisei. The Nisei felt much pressure from their parents to succeed in the United States. Though they were American citizens and had greater facility with the English language, they were subjected to much of the same discrimination that their parents had suffered. To a great extent, the Nisei had dual lives; they went to American public schools during the day and Japanese language schools in the afternoon and on weekends. They also held dual nationalities, because Japan and the United States had different policies for granting citizenship. According to Japanese law, anyone born of a Japanese father is a Japanese citizen; this doctrine is called *jus sanguinis*.

According to U.S. law, anyone born on United States land is an American citizen; this doctrine is called *jus soli*. At the urging of Issei leaders, the Japanese parliament amended their citizenship law in 1916 to allow Issei with children 14 years or younger to renounce their children's Japanese citizenship, and Nisei aged 15 or 16 to renounce their Japanese citizenship on their own. Any male 17 or older, however, had to remain a Japanese citizen until he had completed his military service. In 1924, the Japanese Nationality Act renounced the citizenship of all Nisei. The passage of this Japanese law coincided with the passage in the United States of the 1924 Immigration Act, banning the immigration of all aliens ineligible for citizenship.

Despite the resolution of the citizenship problem, the Nisei continued to be the target of racism. Denied the educational and employment opportunities enjoyed by Americans of European descent, they found it difficult to feel that they belonged in the United States. Yet, they were sufficiently Americanized to feel out of place in Japan as well; most of them did not speak Japanese fluently and were more familiar with American traditions and values than those of Japan.

In addition to the racism they encountered, the Nisei grew up during the Great Depression of the 1930's. Japanese Americans, many of them farmers, struggled to eke out an existence during these hard times. The Nisei adopted one of three strategies to cope with these difficult conditions. In the first strategy, the Nisei saw themselves as interpreters between the Japanese and American cultures, helping the two countries understand each other. These Nisei were closest to the Issei in their philosophy. In the second strategy, Nisei believed it was most important to be patriotic Americans. Nisei who adopted this second strategy believed that they needed to prove themselves constantly as loyal citizens. Proponents of this strategy founded the Japanese American Citizens League. In the third strategy, Nisei identified with other ethnic minorities and became civil rights activists, fighting against racial discrimination.

The outbreak of World War II drastically changed the structure of the Japanese American community. Many Issei community leaders were arrested, both in Hawaii and on the West Coast. The gap was filled by the Nisei, particularly by the pro-American group, the JACL. After the war, the Japanese Americans were dispersed geographically; the U.S. government discouraged the internees from returning to the West Coast for fear of anti-Japanese sentiment. Also after World War II, many of the discriminatory practices against the Japanese were relaxed. Nisei were able to find jobs as teachers, civil servants in local, state, or federal government, and various professional positions in corporations, which were previously unattainable.

The Sansei

The next generation, the Sansei, are almost completely Americanized. The majority of Sansei did not experience the internment during World War II; the discrimination they have encountered has been more subtle. During the 1960's and 1970's, many Sansei were attending university or high school and were exposed to the Civil Rights Movement. Partly as a result of this activist experience, the Sansei joined forces with the Nisei in the 1970's and 1980's to fight for redress and reparations for those interned in camps during World War II. In response to intensive lobbying efforts by the JACL, which served as the umbrella organization for other Japanese American associations during the redress and reparations effort, the U.S. Congress established the Commission on Wartime Relocation and Internment of Civilians. This commission held extensive hearings in 1981 and concluded that the internment was unnecessary and wrong. In 1987 and 1988, the U.S. Congress voted to support an official apology from the federal government and reparations of $20,000 to each internee.

The Yonsei

One of the main changes taking place in the Sansei generation is the high rate of outmarriage. As a result, many Yonsei are

multiracial, which creates a whole new set of issues for the
Japanese American community. In the past, Japanese Americans
were isolated because they were accused of being unable to
assimilate into mainstream society. Their race defined their
ethnicity. Because of the high rate of outmarriage, race is no
longer the main criteria to determine Japanese American
ethnicity. The kinds of discrimination encountered by people of
multiracial origin are, in some ways, more complex. Because
they cannot be so easily pigeonholed, yet are obviously different,
multiracial people are often rejected by all races. The multiracial
Sansei and Yonsei face an identity crisis similar to that
encountered by the Nisei, whose ethnic identities cross two
cultures and nationalities. The Sansei and Yonsei have
multicultural and multiracial ethnic identities; as a result, they
benefit from the richness of their heritage and suffer from the
rigid boundaries built by each race.

3 Immigration: The *Dekasegi* Ideal (1885-1908)

A small group of Japanese came to Hawaii before the large-scale immigration in 1885. In 1868, the first year of the Meiji emperor's reign in Japan, 149 Japanese went to Hawaii to labor under three-year contracts. Their wages were four dollars a month, and their food, lodging, and passage were paid by their employers. All of them were from Yokohama prefecture. Among them were tailors, samurai, cooks, and printers. Known as *gannenmono*, or "first-year people," they were received at first with a great show of hospitality and courtesy while they recovered from the rough sea voyage. After two weeks, they were informed of the plantations to which they were assigned. The friendliness that greeted them off the ship was replaced by the backbreaking labor and strict discipline of plantation life. The *gannenmono* were not used to such treatment and began to complain before the end of the first month. The plantation owners were also unhappy; when one worker collapsed in the field and later died, an unsympathetic planter demanded a full refund and described how the man's collapse had resulted in delays because other laborers had to take care of him. After negotiations between Japan and Hawaii, forty Japanese were permitted to return to Japan before their three-year contract had

ended. Thirteen more returned at the end of the three years, and
the rest stayed in Hawaii. The Japanese government viewed the
whole affair as a disaster. As a result, Japan banned emigration
altogether and broke off friendly relations with Hawaii. Two
years later, the two governments signed a treaty restoring their
friendship.

In 1876, the Kingdom of Hawaii signed a treaty with the
United States regarding sugar production and trade. In order to
meet American demand, Hawaii had to increase the amount of
sugar it produced. Beginning in 1881, Hawaii tried to convince
Japan to allow its citizens to work overseas. The plantation
owners and government leaders in Hawaii were unhappy with the
large population of Chinese immigrants; Japanese labor, it was
hoped, would reduce the importance of Chinese workers. In fact,
the year after the Japanese began arriving in Hawaii, Chinese
immigration to Hawaii ended.

In Japan, the economy was in bad shape. More than 300,000
farmers lost their land. Typhoons and other natural disasters
further destroyed the countryside. Unable to find jobs, many
Japanese jumped at the first chance to work, even if they had to
leave their families and country. The idea of leaving their native
village to find temporary work was not new to Japanese. Known
as *dekasegi,* this concept was practiced widely in Japan. Three
concepts made up the *dekasegi* ideal. First, considering *dekasegi*
meant that a person was empty-handed (*toshu kuken*). Second, a
person hoped to strike it rich immediately (*ikkaku senki*). Finally,
having done so, the person would return home with his newfound
wealth (*kin'i kikyo*).

The difficult conditions suffered by many Japanese made
dekasegi even more attractive. When the Japanese government
announced that there were 950 openings for the first ship to
Hawaii, the *City of Tokyo*, it received 28,000 applications. The
City of Tokyo arrived in Honolulu in February, 1885, carrying
676 men, 159 women, and 108 children. Like the *gannenmono*,
these immigrants had three-year contracts. Their wages were nine
dollars a month for men and six dollars a month for women.

They had to work 26 days each month, ten hours a day for field workers and twelve for mill workers.

By 1894, a total of about 29,000 contract laborers had immigrated to Hawaii. From 1894 to 1908, another 125,000 arrived. The group that came between 1885 and 1894 were overseen by the Japanese government and were called *kanyaku imin*. Private companies took over emigration in 1894 and turned it into a huge profit-making business, at the expense of the emigrants. Often, these emigrants, known as *jiyu imin*, had to take loans from the emigration companies, which charged high interest rates. An immigrant named Ko Shigeta came to Hawaii in 1903 when he was seventeen years old. He had borrowed 100 yen from a bank owned by three emigration companies. He earned fourteen dollars a month for working nine hours a day, seven days a week. He paid seven or eight dollars a month rent to live with fifty other laborers in a ten-foot wide shed. It took him two years to pay back the loan.

Contract Labor

For the contract laborers, life on the plantations was very hard. In addition to the long hours and meager pay, the overseers, called *lunas*, were often cruel. The *lunas* ruled by fear. They enforced strict rules by holding back wages, fining, putting the workers in prison, and beating them. The *lunas* were supported by the plantation owners, the courts, and the police. The workers had no rights. Although lynching and other forms of extreme violence were rare, they did occur. In 1889, the body of a Japanese merchant named Hiroshi Goto was found hanging from a telephone pole. Goto had spoken out in favor of the rights of Japanese laborers. The five *lunas* charged with the murder were found guilty. When they stated that they were going to appeal, they were released from jail on bail. They immediately left Hawaii and never served their sentences.

Women had an especially difficult time, since they not only worked in the fields but also cleaned and cooked for their husbands and families at the beginning and end of each day. Pregnant women worked up to the day they delivered and took their babies with them to the fields. Since they were far outnumbered by the men, women were both isolated from other women and harassed by men.

Despite their fear, Japanese workers did protest the conditions under which they worked. There were numerous strikes, which protested the cruelty of *lunas*, low wages, the wrongful arrest of a laborer, and unreasonable rules. In April, 1891, 150 workers in Hana, Maui, walked off the fields to protest not being paid. In June, 1893, all 250 workers at Kukuihaele, Hawaii, marched to town to watch the trial of a *luna* who had shot and wounded a Japanese who had supposedly attacked him with a knife. In March, 1897, 200 workers went on strike when two fellow workers were arrested for refusing to work.

In 1898, the United States annexed Hawaii, making it an American territory. In 1900, the United States government passed the Organic Act, which made all United States laws applicable in

Little Tokyo, in Los Angeles; most of the early Japanese immigrants settled on the West Coast or Hawaii. (David Fowler)

Hawaii. As a result, labor contracts became illegal, and many
Japanese were no longer bound to the plantations. Those who
stayed on the plantations began to organize themselves to fight for
their rights. In 1900, there were more than twenty strikes,
involving a total of 7,800 workers. The largest strike included
1,350 workers. One of the most important strikes took place in
1904 on the Waipahu plantation. For four days strikers refused to
work, demanding that the head *luna*, named Patterson, be fired.
Patterson had created a lottery, and he sold tickets to workers for
a dollar a ticket. If they refused to buy the tickets, the workers
were punished. Because of the strike, Patterson was fired and
gambling was ended. In May, 1905, 1,400 Japanese workers in
Lahaina, Maui, protested the blinding of a fellow laborer by a
luna. During the protest, local police fired on the strikers, killing
one and wounding two or three. About 150 police, both local and
from other islands, amassed in Lahaina to end the strike. As they
had with the Chinese, government leaders and plantation owners
were beginning to feel overwhelmed by the large Japanese
population and felt that their personal safety was at risk.

Other Early Immigrants

On the West Coast of the United States, the arrival of large
numbers of Japanese laborers was preceded by two smaller
groups of immigrants: student-laborers, or *dekasegi-shosei*, and
prostitutes. Although there were a few Japanese students who
were wealthy enough to attend prestigious universities on the
East Coast, the majority split their time between working and
studying, mostly in San Francisco. The *dekasegi-shosei* came to
the United States for several reasons: to learn English and a skill
that would help them start a successful career in Japan, to avoid
being drafted into the military, or to escape political persecution.

The students struggled to make ends meet and learn English.
Many of them found jobs as household servants, which was very
humiliating for them. By 1890, there were approximately 2,500

dekasegi-shosei in the United States; another 2,500 came between 1891 and 1900. Few of them finished school or returned to Japan. Instead, the *dekasegi-shosei* established Christian institutions and newspapers, thereby providing the basis for an immigrant society. Many of them became labor-contractors and immigrant leaders.

The Japanese prostitutes had been arriving in the United States since 1861. Poor families in rural Japan sold their daughters to agents of companies that supposedly specialized in domestic services. Other women were kidnaped or lured from their home by false promises of high wages. These women were sent directly to the United States or went through China and Southeast Asia. Once they arrived in the United States, they were put to work in brothels.

The Demand for Japanese Workers

In 1882, the United States government had passed the Chinese Exclusion Law, which prevented Chinese from emigrating to the United States for ten years. Chinese exclusion was extended for another ten years in 1902 and then extended indefinitely in 1904. By the end of the 1880's, railroad companies, lumber mills, and farmers on the West Coast needed a new source of cheap labor to replace the aging Chinese workers. Like Hawaii, the West Coast states looked to Japan. Between 1891 and 1900, more than 27,000 Japanese arrived in the United States. With the annexation of Hawaii in 1898 and the end of contract labor in 1900, West Coast employers also recruited from the new territory. Between 1901 and 1907 more than 80,000 Japanese came to the mainland: 42,000 from Japan and 38,000 from Hawaii.

The Japanese workers who came to the West Coast were employed by contractors, who held agreements with companies needing cheap labor. The contractors were usually Japanese and had been in the United States long enough to learn English and get connections. All labor disputes were handled by the contractor. The contractor charged the laborers for food and lodging, as well as other miscellaneous services such as a medical clinic. As a result, the contractors became very rich. Like the emigration companies in Hawaii, their wealth was accumulated at the expense of the laborers.

The arrival of large numbers of Japanese immigrants to the West Coast occurred at the same time as the rise of the American Federation of Labor (AFL), which represented the rights of workers in the United States. Headed by Samuel Gompers, the AFL was a major proponent of Japanese exclusion. According to the AFL, Japanese immigrants worked for lower wages than European workers and had a low standard of living; as a result, they lowered the standard of living of white workers who competed with them. The AFL also stated that the Japanese could not become unionized because they were controlled by the contractors. The AFL continued its racist exclusion policy until the 1930's.

Japanese Organized Labor

Yet the Japanese did organize themselves. In 1892, for example, Japanese shoemakers in San Francisco formed the Japanese Shoemakers' League in response to hostility from the Boot and Shoemakers' White Labor League to their presence. In order to avoid competing the white shoemakers, the Japanese specialized in repairing rather than making shoes. The Japanese Shoemakers' League began with 20 members and eventually peaked at 327 in 1909. The League had strict rules regarding membership, location of shops, and the opening of new shops. The League also created a business fund, from which members could borrow to start a new shop or expand an existing one.

In 1903, Japanese and Mexican laborers in Oxnard, California, went on strike. They formed the Japanese-Mexican Labor Association (JMLA) and stated their demands. First, the Western Agricultural Contracting Company (WACC) was not paying the

A mall in San Francisco's Japantown; the Japanese American community in San Francisco has deep roots. (Kimberly Dawson)

workers what they had been promised. Second, the JMLA protested the WACC's use of subcontractors, because laborers were charged both by the subcontractors and the WACC. Third, the workers wanted to end the WACC policy of forcing them to buy at WACC stores, which charged high prices. At the beginning of March, 90 percent of the workers were on strike. By the end of March, the WACC had canceled all but one of its contracts with the farms in the area. The JMLA had broken the WACC monopoly on contracting and had ended the subcontracting system. After their success, the JMLA petitioned the AFL to become a member. Gompers agreed to accept the JMLA only if no Japanese or Chinese were allowed. Refusing to join on such a condition, the JMLA eventually disbanded.

Growing Anti-Japanese Sentiment

Anti-Asian groups on the West Coast became alarmed at the numbers of Japanese immigrants. In May, 1900, local labor groups organized a mass anti-Japanese protest in San Francisco. Among the supporters of the demonstration was the city mayor, James Phelan. The AFL began pushing for exclusion of all Asians from the country. All major political parties in California took anti-Japanese stands.

In 1905, the Japanese defeated the Russians after a two years of fierce battles. The rest of world had to recognize the growing military might of the Japanese. American newspapers adopted anti-Japanese positions, stirring up fears about Japan's intentions toward the United States and the role of the resident Japanese. Popular films and novels of the period presented Japanese as sneaky, cunning, and fanatically loyal to the emperor. In 1905, the Japanese and Korean Exclusion League, later called the Asiatic Exclusion League, was formed. By 1908, it had more than 100,000 members.

In December 1906, the San Francisco school board ordered all school principals to send Chinese, Japanese, and Korean children to Asian schools. At the time, there were less than one hundred Japanese children in public schools in San Francisco. The Japanese government protested the school board's actions to Washington, D.C. Wanting to avoid confrontation with Japan, President Theodore Roosevelt sent for the mayor of San Francisco and the school board members. In his discussions with the San Francisco delegation, Roosevelt discovered that the segregation order was part of a strategy to get the attention of Washington and push the government toward preventing any further immigration from Japan.

Although President Roosevelt protested the school board's decision and convinced the school board to repeal it, it was clear that he agreed with them about immigration. In March, 1907, he handed down an executive order to prevent any aliens from entering the continental United States whose passports were issued for places other than the mainland, such as Canada, Hawaii, or Mexico. This order halted almost all Japanese migration from Hawaii. At the end of 1907, the United States government began negotiating with Japan to end the migration of laborers to the United States and Hawaii. Negotiations were completed in the summer of 1908 and what was known as the Gentlemen's Agreement went into effect immediately.

The Japanese immigrants who came to the United States had few choices in resisting the discrimination they faced. Unable to become citizens, they had none of these rights. Instead, they had to rely on the Japanese government to support them through diplomacy, go through the court system to protest unfair laws, and try to appeal to the American's sense of justice. Unfortunately, the Japanese government time and time again sacrificed the welfare of the Japanese immigrants to maintain good relations with the United States. The American sense of justice was smothered by racist, anti-Japanese feelings. Abandoned by the Japanese government and unwelcomed by the American people, the Japanese immigrants saw the courts as their only salvation. As described in the next chapter, they were disappointed.

4 Permanent Settlement: *Dochaku Eiju* (1909-1940)

After the Gentlemen's Agreement was signed in 1908, the leaders of the Japanese community in the United States and Hawaii began to rethink the *dekasegi* idea. The immigrants felt that the Japanese government had given in to American pressure and had sacrificed their welfare for international relations. The term they applied to themselves was *kimin*, or abandoned people. Since they lacked support from home, immigrant leaders decided to encourage the idea of permanent settlement, or *dochaku eiju*.

One of the leaders on the mainland who favored this idea was Kyutaro Abiko. Abiko published one of the most influential immigrant newspapers, *Nichibei Shimbun*. According to Abiko, the *dekasegi* attitude was the main obstacle to making the good qualities of the Issei more apparent to white Americans. By shedding the attitude that their stay was temporary, Japanese immigrants would try to improve their living standards and create a stable community. Abiko realized that Japanese immigrants needed to have a stake in the country, and he encouraged his countrymen to invest in land. He also urged them to send for wives from Japan and start families. Abiko believed that family life would reduce some of the more unattractive aspects of immigrant life, such as gambling, prostitution, and drinking.

In many cases, the land that the Issei bought, leased, or contracted was very poor. With hard work, they transformed the previously barren acres into lush, productive farmland. Perhaps the biggest success story was that of Kinji Ushijima, known as George Shima, the "Potato King." Shima started out as a potato picker in the San Joaquin Valley of central California. After becoming a labor contractor, he decided to become a farmer. He started by leasing fifteen acres. He then leased and bought nearby swamplands, drained them, and converted them into potato fields. By 1912, Shima owned 10,000 acres of potatoes, in addition to owning enough steamboats to ship his crops from Stockton to San Francisco. He defied racists in Berkeley when he settled in a house there, despite protests from newspapers and neighbors. When he died in 1926, his estate was worth $15 million.

Shima was an exception. Most immigrants worked on small parcels of land. The Gentlemen's Agreement prohibited the immigration of Japanese laborers, but farmers and businessmen were allowed to send for wives and relatives. Many Issei looked to their wives and future children as prospective workers. From 1910 to 1920, more than twenty thousand Japanese women arrived in the United States. Most of them were picture brides. The marriage had been arranged by the families, and the couple knew each other only by photograph.

Often the brides were disappointed by both their husbands and their homes. In order to attract a wife, many Issei touched up their photographs to make them look younger. They also played down or did not mention the often primitive conditions in which they lived. As in Hawaii, the wives had to work very hard. They took care of the house and worked in the fields. Their husbands were usually older than they were and more conservative. There were instances of women deserting their husbands. Despite suffering many hardships, however, most women did not desert their husbands. In fact, by 1920, almost thirty thousand Nisei children had been born. With the arrival of the picture brides and the establishment of families, the Japanese community changed.

Japanese Associations

In 1908, the Japanese Association of America was created. This organization was connected to the Japanese government. It had a central office in San Francisco. Under the central office were regional associations, such as the Northwest American Japanese Association in the Pacific Northwest. These regional associations were further broken down into local associations. The associations were authorized by the Japanese government to process applications for birth, death, marriage, and divorce certificates; for travel to and from the United States; and for draft registration, among other things. Through their power to issue these certificates, the local associations were able to control the behavior of the Japanese population. Applications from undesirables such as gamblers and prostitutes were denied. Moreover, since the local associations were connected to the regional and central associations, a person whose application was refused would find it difficult to be accepted anywhere. In this way, the Japanese associations tried to cultivate an immigrant community that was acceptable to the larger society, weeding out the bad elements.

Through the Japanese associations, the Issei made important business connections. One example is the rotating credit association. A group of Issei would pool their money together in order to make loans to each other. This type of loan would enable the cash-poor immigrants to buy or lease land or start a business.

The Anti-Japanese Movement

What Abiko and other leaders did not realize is that the American white majority did not want the Japanese, no matter how many American customs they adopted. In fact, the anti-Japanese exclusionists viewed the Japanese as even more dangerous than the Chinese because the former wore Western clothes and tried to become Americanized. According to the anti-Japanese movement, the Japanese could never assimilate. The last thing the exclusionists wanted was to have the Japanese settling down and having children.

Beginning in 1907, leaders of the anti-Japanese movement began working to pass anti-Japanese legislation in the California state legislature concerning property, education, and immigration. In 1913, the Alien Land Law was passed. This law prohibited the ownership of land by aliens ineligible for citizenship. The Issei fell in this category, as a result of a law passed in 1790 by Congress, which restricted the right of citizenship by naturalization to "free white" persons. Fortunately for Issei, there were loopholes in the land law. For example, the Issei were able to place the title to the land in their American-born child's name; as parents, they served as guardians. They also created corporations in which they were not the majority shareholders to purchase the land.

The anti-Japanese movement quickly became aware of the loopholes and began lobbying to amend the land law. In 1920, the California state legislature passed a tougher version of the 1913 law, and many Issei lost their land. That same year, a law was passed banning the further migration of picture brides. In response to the land laws, the Japanese community decided to test both the validity and applicability of the laws. Several cases were brought to court questioning the constitutionality of the law itself. Other cases tested the naturalization issue.

The Ozawa Case

In 1913, the Japanese Association of America had created an organization called the Pacific Coast Japanese Association Deliberative Council, which was tasked with solving some of the

Like this musician playing the koto during the Cherry Blossom festival, many Japanese Americans have preserved elements of their traditional culture. (David Young-Wolff/ PhotoEdit)

broader problems faced by the Japanese community. One of the issues was naturalization. In order to go to court, the council needed an ideal candidate. The case of Takao Ozawa came to the council's attention in 1917. Ozawa had come to the United States at age nineteen, was graduated from high school in California, attended University of California for three years, then moved to Honolulu. He worked for an American company and was married with two children. He did not belong to any Japanese organizations, his children attended American schools and churches, and he spoke mostly English at home. Finally, he did not smoke, drink, or gamble.

Ozawa filed for naturalization in October, 1914. His petition was rejected. He took his case to court. The lower courts ruled that since he was a member of the "Mongolian" race, he was not a "free white person" and therefore could not become a citizen. Ozawa appealed to a higher court, which passed the case on to the Supreme Court without making a ruling on it. It was at this point that the Pacific Coast Japanese Association Deliberative Council became aware of Ozawa's efforts and decided to support him.

Ozawa's case split the community. Some believed that the Japanese Association should not support Ozawa, since the Japanese government had expressed its disapproval of the case. Furthermore, a snag came up in Ozawa's case; more than seven years had passed between when he filed for petition of intent to naturalize and when he filed for naturalization. As a result, the *Nichibei Shimbun*, Abiko's paper, withdrew its support of the case. Other newspapers increased their support of Ozawa in response to Abiko's decision, and an often-bitter debate was started.

Meanwhile, the Supreme Court delayed taking up the case for international reasons. World War I was coming to a close. Japan had sided with the Allies and was attending the peace treaty discussions. Arms limitation negotiations followed the peace treaty and further delayed hearing the case. In 1922, the Supreme Court finally took up the case. The judges decided to ignore the discrepancy in years between the intent to file and the actual filing, and ruled on the case. The court determined that Ozawa was neither a free white person nor an African; therefore, he could not become naturalized. Most of the community was not surprised at the Supreme Court's decision. At least the issue was now at rest. Japanese immigrants had no political power in the United States.

Alien Land Laws

The cases that concerned the alien land laws had a more practical impact on the community. The 1920 amendment to the 1913 Alien Land Law was designed to drive the Japanese out of farming, except in the positions at which they started - field laborers. The Issei were not allowed to lease land, appoint themselves guardians of land held by minors, or hold stock in companies that owned land. If the law was enforced, Japanese farmers could lose close to 100,000 acres of currently leased land. The cases that went to court tested several aspects of the land laws. In every case, the Supreme Court ruled against the Japanese. The Japanese community was devastated. The economic foundation of the community, agriculture, had been destroyed. Unable to get loans to pay outstanding debts, thousands of farmers lost their land. In 1918, there had been almost 8,000 Japanese farmers. By 1929, there were approximately 4,500. As a result of the Supreme Court rulings, the Japanese community leaders began to consider leaving the country or the Western states. Yet, the majority stayed. They had invested too much time and money to start over, and they had families to support.

The Immigration Act of 1924

The final, most painful legislation passed by the United States Congress was the 1924 Immigration Act, which ended all

Japanese immigration. As if denying them naturalization rights and taking their land away was not enough, the United States government had to push the humiliation even further. The Issei were completely cut off from their home country. In addition, more than 20,000 Issei bachelors had no hope of becoming married and having children. As they tried to make the best of a bad situation, their struggle to make a home in a hostile country was made worse by the Great Depression. Anti-Japanese hostility increased as more white Americans lost jobs. There were a number of cases of anti-Japanese violence in Central California shortly after the Immigration Act went into effect on July 1, 1924.

Responses to Discrimination

All of the anti-Japanese legislation was psychologically damaging to the Japanese. The lesson they learned was that no matter how they tried to assimilate and adopt American customs and culture, they were not wanted. The Japanese community faced a contradictory situation. They were accused by the white majority of being incapable of assimilating, yet it was the very same majority that prevented them from assimilating. A similar and more tragic irony would take place during World War II, when the Issei were labeled as enemy aliens, a status that the United States had imposed on them by preventing them from becoming citizens.

In general, the Japanese were very successful farmers and businessmen. Through hard work and some innovative techniques, they had reclaimed land that others had deemed unusable. They worked longer hours than their white counterparts and were willing to live with fewer material possessions. The Issei sacrificed the pleasures of life for the future of their children. With the passage of the anti-Japanese legislation, it became even more clear that the future of the Japanese community lay with the Nisei, not the Issei.

The Issei placed high importance on the education of their children, the Nisei. As a result, many Nisei were better educated than whites. Because of discrimination, however, the Nisei were unable to get jobs that matched their education. Trained as teachers or doctors, many ended up working in the family business or on the farm. Moreover, although the Nisei attended public, integrated schools, they did not socialize with Caucasians. Some Nisei recall not being allowed to swim in the local swimming pool and not being served at restaurants. They were taunted and beat up by their white classmates.

The Nisei responded in several ways to the discrimination they faced. Some were discouraged and resigned themselves to a life of menial labor. They saw no reason to get an education when they would spend their days working in a fruitstand. Other Nisei tried to fight the discrimination as voters. In California, they created Japanese-American Democratic Clubs in San Francisco, Oakland, and Los Angeles. In addition to supporting the New Deal and liberal Democratic candidates, they championed legislation that banned racial discrimination. They passed out petitions and attended Democratic meetings. Most of them were from the working class, and were trying to achieve equal opportunity and treatment in their jobs.

One of the most significant responses to racial discrimination was the formation of the Japanese American Citizens League (JACL) in 1930. Whereas the Japanese-American Democratic Clubs were composed mostly of working class Nisei, the JACL was started by Nisei professionals and businessmen. James Sakamoto was one of the founders of the JACL. He emphasized that the Nisei had to be "one hundred percent Americans" in order to be treated as such. From the beginning, the JACL was conceived as a national organization. The JACL was similar to the Japanese Associations of the Issei in that both organizations tried to educate the rest of American society about the Japanese community and served as the focal point for the community itself. The major difference between the JACL and Japanese Associations was the relationship to Japan. The Japanese Associations linked the Japanese immigrant community to the Japanese government. The JACL had no such link.

Japanese Americans have always placed a high value on education. (Michael Newman/PhotoEdit)

The JACL also differed from the Democratic Clubs in their approach to improving the Nisei's position in society. The JACL believed that politics was too militant. The key to acceptance was loyalty. Sakamoto stated: "Instead of worrying about anti-Japanese activity or legislation, we must exert our efforts to building the abilities and character of the second generation so they will become loyal and useful citizens who, some day, will make their contribution to the greatness of American life."

In Hawaii, the Japanese faced hostility that had its roots in a different but equally racist soil. Planters feared that the Japanese had become too strong; their ability to strike, especially after the strike of 1920, was seen as a threat to the planters' domination. After the strike, the planters developed several strategies to deal with the Japanese. They tried to get U.S. Congress to allow Chinese to immigrate to Hawaii. Congress had extended the Chinese Exclusion Act since 1882. Through their territorial representatives, the planters painted a picture of the Japanese menace. The Japanese became not only a labor problem but a military problem. By adding military necessity, the planters broadened the appeal of their request. However, they faced the opposition of West Coast politicians, labor unions, and newspapers, who were strongly anti-Asian. Whereas many Japanese viewed the 1920 strike as a class struggle, the planters depicted it as a show of ethnic and racial force. The planters were unsuccessful in their bid to sidestep the Chinese Exclusion Act. Their legislation was bogged down in Congress and never made it to a floor discussion. Through their efforts, however, military surveillance of the Japanese was increased, and the Japanese problem became a national issue.

Failing in their efforts to dilute the concentration of Japanese, the planters managed to pass territorial legislation that defined strikes as a type of terrorism and made the action punishable. Japanese language newspapers also became targets; they were defined as printing material that caused dissension among different races. Similar laws were passed against picketing and union-organizing meetings.

Having clamped down on labor, Hawaii's leaders took on the Americanization of the Japanese. Buddhism and Japanese language schools came under attack. Buddhism was described in the local newspapers as profoundly un-American and undemocratic. Hawaiian legislators passed laws strictly regulating the language schools. Teachers had to be certified and tested for the knowledge of American history and the English language. Textbooks and the curriculum were also examined for their American content. In addition, the first three years of Japanese language school education, from kindergarten to second grade, was abolished.

In public schools, the children of plantation laborers were encouraged to go into vocational training, with an emphasis on producing a new generation of efficient workers. Schools were segregated. Those with mostly Asian students attended agricultural and housekeeping classes. Those with mostly white students attended classes preparing them for university and professional careers.

In essence, the Japanese were being blamed for being Japanese. Although they were told to adopt American customs and ideals, they were accused of being incapable of assimilating. While the American ideal of equal opportunity was being ingrained in their minds, they were being accused of being too ambitious, of being dissatisfied workers, because they did not want to go back to the plantations.

It was into this atmosphere of intense anti-Japanese feelings that World War II became a reality for the United States. On December 7, 1941, Japanese planes flew into Pearl Harbor.

5 The Incarceration (1941-1945)

On December 8, 1941, the United States declared war on Japan. According to the 1940 census, there were 285,115 persons of Japanese ancestry living in the United States, including Hawaii and Alaska. More than two-thirds were American citizens. Months before Japan bombed Pearl Harbor, a special investigator named Curtis Munson was sent to Hawaii and the West Coast states by the State Department. Munson's job was to assess the loyalty of the Japanese community. His investigation took place from the beginning of October through the first weeks of November, 1941.

In his twenty-five page report, Munson found that his findings agreed with current military intelligence. "There is no Japanese 'problem' on the Coast," he concluded. "There will be no armed uprising of Japanese. There will undoubtedly be some sabotage financed by Japan and executed largely by imported agents. . . . For the most part the local Japanese are loyal to the United States or, at worst, hope that by remaining quiet they can avoid concentration camps or irresponsible mobs. We do not believe that they would be at the least any more disloyal than any other racial group in the United States with whom we went to war."

In Hawaii, Munson again concluded that the Japanese were not a problem, despite their large population. "The consensus of opinion is that there will be no racial uprising of the Japanese in Honolulu. The first generation, as on the Coast, are ideologically

41

and culturally closest to Japan. Though many of them speak no English, or at best only pigeon-English, it is considered that the big bulk of them will be loyal. . . . The second generation is estimated as approximately 98 percent loyal."

Military intelligence in both Hawaii and on the West Coast had come up with a list of residents who posed a security risk. When Pearl Harbor was bombed, however, hysteria prevailed over more rational plans. The Secretary of the Navy Frank Knox made matters worse on the West Coast when he held a press conference in Los Angeles on December 15, 1941, after a brief inspection of Pearl Harbor. He spoke of the treachery that took place in Hawaii and stated that much of the damage had been caused by saboteurs. In fact, the level of damage at Pearl Harbor was the result of military incompetence and lack of readiness, and Knox knew that when he made his statement to the press.

In Hawaii, there were about 157,000 people of Japanese ancestry living in Hawaii out of a total population of 421,000. Of the 157,000, 35,000 were aliens and 68,000 held dual citizenship; the remainder were American citizens only. The military first started making plans in case of an attack by Japan in the 1920's. Since then, the plan had undergone several revisions, taking into account new information from intelligence reports, particularly about the loyalty of the Japanese community on Oahu. The military had considered several options, including sending them all to the mainland to concentration camps, to one of the smaller and more remote Hawaiian islands such as Molokai, and to camps in the Oahu valley. Because the Japanese made up more than one-third of the population on Hawaii and were an essential part of the economy, however, none of these options was considered practical or possible. From its intelligence work, the military had determined that about 600 people, most of them of Japanese background, represented a security threat.

Martial law was declared on the day of the attack and lasted until October 24, 1944. The whole population of Hawaii was under the control of the military. From October 24, 1944, to October 24, 1945, the military returned most government functions back to the civilians, except for security and military aspects. On October 24, 1945, all government authority was returned to the civilians. During the almost four-year period of military authority, about 10,000 people living on the islands were investigated as possible security threats. The number of Japanese who were interned as a result of the investigations was 1,250. Thus, the overwhelming majority of the Japanese population living on the islands was allowed to continue living in their homes.

Although everyone living in Hawaii was subjected to curfew, travel, and rationing restrictions, the Japanese community had more severe rules to follow. For example, the Japanese had to turn in any weapons, they had to register as aliens, their curfews were longer, and their travel routes were shorter. Moreover, the Japanese fishing industry was completely shut down.

Directly after the attack, the FBI and the military began arresting those on their suspect list. On December 8, 1941, the Sand Island Detention Camp became the holding place for those arrested. Sand Island was used for fifteen months.

Throughout December, January, and February, the Federal Bureau of Investigation arrested about 3,000 mainland Issei and took radios and cameras from Japanese homes. Nisei who had registered with the military were placed in the same class as enemy aliens. Those in the military were either discharged or given menial positions. West Coast politicians, newspapers, and labor unions urged the government to remove all Japanese from the West Coast. In California, all state employees of Japanese ancestry were laid off.

In February, the army named twelve restricted areas. Enemy aliens living in these areas were not allowed to be out of their homes from 9 p.m. to 6 a.m. During the day their movements were restricted to going from their home to work and back. Furthermore, they were not allowed to travel more than five miles from their home.

The beginning of the incarceration. (National Archives)

Executive Order 9066

On February 19, President Franklin Roosevelt signed Executive Order 9066, in which he authorized the Secretary of War to establish military areas and exclude anyone from these areas. The next day, Secretary of War Henry Stimson appointed Lieutenant General John L. DeWitt in charge of carrying out the executive order. DeWitt was a career military officer who had never been in combat. His fellow officers had little respect for his judgment. In fact, DeWitt allowed himself to be influenced more by politicians and businessmen than by military intelligence reports.

Among those who influenced DeWitt was then-Attorney General of California Earl Warren. Warren was a member of the Native Sons of the Golden West, one of the most vocal anti-Japanese groups in California. He was also planning to run for governor in November, 1941. Warren argued that the Japanese farmers had chosen the location of their farms for strategic purposes. As evidence, he pointed out the sinister location of Japanese-owned or run farms near airports, railroad lines, power stations, and dams. According to Warren, this was not coincidence. Furthermore, Warren stated that there was no way to test the loyalty of the Japanese, alien or American. He even stated that the Nisei were more dangerous than the Issei. Warren urged that all persons of Japanese ancestry be removed from the West Coast.

Warren's statements may be understood in the context of the anti-Japanese movement that had been growing since the late 1800's. He did not have access to military intelligence reports, such as the Munson Report. Rather than relying on the content of the Munson report, the Army used a twisted logic to support its evacuation plans. In arguing the military necessity of the evacuation, DeWitt stated "the very fact that no sabotage has taken place to date is a disturbing and confirming indication that such action will be taken." He also pointed to the surprise attack on Pearl Harbor as evidence that the Japanese saboteurs were simply waiting for the Americans to relax their guard.

Under pressure from local politicians and the press and the military in Washington, D.C., DeWitt began taking action. On February 28, DeWitt made Washington, Oregon, California, and parts of Arizona military areas 1 and 2. On March 16, DeWitt made Idaho, Montana, Nevada, and Utah military areas 3 through 6. Two days later, President Roosevelt signed Executive Order 9102, which created the War Relocation Authority (WRA). The WRA's task was to put together a program to evacuate

people from the military areas. On March 21, congress passed a
law that provided for punishment of those who violated laws to
enter or leave the military areas. With that backing from the
President and Congress, Dewitt began issuing a series of
exclusion orders for all Japanese aliens and "nonaliens" from the
military areas. Using this kind of terminology, the U.S.
government conferred on the Nisei a new status - neither alien
nor citizen.

———————

Incarceration

During this time, the WRA established fifteen assembly
centers, usually converted race tracks or fair grounds. The
Japanese were taken to the assembly centers while permanent
"relocation centers" were being built. In this book, the term
"concentration camp" is used to describe the camps administered
by the WRA. "Internment camp" refers specifically to the camps
run by the Justice Department. "Relocation center" or camp,
which is preferred by the government, is too easily confused with
the initial voluntary relocation policy attempted by the army and
with the relocation program that followed the closing of the
camps. It is also worth noting that President Roosevelt and other
government officials referred to the camps as concentration
camps. The ten concentration camps were located in inhospitable
parts of the country, such as the desert or swampland.

Of the 157,905 living in Hawaii, 1,875 were taken to the
mainland and placed in concentration camps or internment
camps, and 1,466 were placed in concentration camps in Hawaii.
From the mainland, 110,723 Japanese aliens and Americans were
sent to concentration camps.

Since many Issei were arrested, the Nisei were forced to fill in
the leadership gap. The JACL, with its pro-American stance,
quickly appointed itself spokesperson for the community. JACL
leaders such as Mike Masaoka came to the conclusion that the
only way to prove their loyalty to the United States was to obey

all orders without question. In fact, Masaoka offered the idea of allowing Nisei volunteers to go on suicide missions while their Issei parents were held as hostages. The idea was rejected at the time. The idea of Nisei volunteers would find its shape in the all-Nisei combat team.

Resistance

Although the majority of Japanese did go to the camps without a fight, some refused, including three Nisei: Gordon Hirabayashi, Fred Korematsu, and Minoru Yasui. Hirabayashi was a student at the University of Washington when he decided to refuse to obey both the curfew and evacuation orders. Hirabayashi was a Quaker. Through his church connections, Hirabayashi was contacted by lawyers from the American Civil Liberties Union (ACLU). The ACLU wanted to test the constitutionality of the evacuation orders. Korematsu was a welder in Los Angeles. He tried to conceal his Japanese ancestry by getting plastic surgery and pretending to be Spanish-Hawaiian. When he was caught, he was also contacted by lawyers from the ACLU, who wanted to use his case to test the evacuation orders. Korematsu agreed. Yasui was a lawyer from Oregon. He believed that the curfew order was unconstitutional and decided to test it in the courts.

All three cases eventually went to the United States Supreme Court, and all were convicted. The rulings on Hirabayashi's and Yasui's cases were announced together in April, 1943. In Hirabayashi's case, the Supreme Court avoided ruling on the evacuation order, because of technicalities. They did rule on Hirabayashi's violation of the curfew. The judges relied on information presented by Justice Department lawyers that the Japanese Americans were a dangerous presence on the West Coast. Hirabayashi spent all of the war years in jail. First he was in King County Jail in Seattle, Washington, then in a federal prison in Tucson, Arizona, and finally in a federal penitentiary on McNeil Island.

Yasui's case was peculiar because of a lower court judge's ruling. Judge Fee stated that Yasui had given up his citizenship rights by working for the Japanese consulate in Chicago, Illinois. Judge Fee also ruled that the curfew order was unconstitutional as it applied to American citizens. Since Yasui was no longer a citizen, this ruling did not apply to him. When Yasui's case arrived at the Supreme Court, the justices decided that Judge Fee had ruled incorrectly on Yasui's citizenship status and on the curfew order. As a result, the Supreme Court sent the case back to Judge Fee for resentencing based on the higher court's findings. Yasui had already spent nine months in solitary confinement and was incarcerated at the Minidoka concentration camp in Idaho at the time of the Supreme Court's decision. Judge Fee resentenced Yasui to the nine months that he had already served, and Yasui was taken back to Minidoka. He became active with the JACL and counseled those who refused to register for the draft.

The decision on Korematsu's case was made public on December 18, 1944, along with that on a fourth case brought by the ACLU in the name of Mitsuye Endo. Unlike the others, Endo had reported to the Tanforan Assembly Center, and then filed her suit from there. Her case differed from the other three in that she was asking that the court require the War Relocation Authority to show proof that she should not be released. The WRA offered to release her if she agreed not to return to the West Coast, but Endo refused to drop the case and spent the next two years in Topaz, Utah.

Whereas the Supreme Court justices avoided ruling on the evacuation order in the Hirabayashi and Yasui cases and were able to maintain unanimity, the Korematsu case divided the court sharply. Although they were not actually ruling on the constitutionality of the incarceration, it became the main issue. The divisions can partly be attributed to courtroom politics and partly to the status of the war, which had begun turning in the favor of the Americans. Thus, the military necessity of the incarceration was less justified. Those justices who had earlier silenced their doubts in the Hirabayashi and Yasui cases in order to present a united front were compelled to voice their dissent. The majority opinion stated that the decision to evacuate the Japanese population was based on national defense, not racial prejudice. In his dissent, Justice Frank Murphy pointed his finger at racism as the culprit in the evacuation order. He cited Austin Anson, one of the leaders of the Salinas Vegetable Grower-Shipper Association, who said, "We're charged with wanting to get rid of the Japs for selfish reasons. We do. It's a question of whether the white man lives on the Pacific Coast or the brown men." To Murphy, the Supreme Court conviction of Korematsu represented the "legalization of racism." Meanwhile, Korematsu was working in Detroit, Michigan, as a welder. After being led from his first court hearing at gunpoint, Korematsu had been sent to Minidoka. He later got out and found work in Detroit.

In Mitsuye Endo's case, the Supreme Court ruled that the government could not detain a citizen whose loyalty had been determined. The Supreme Court handed down their rulings on the Endo and Korematsu cases the day after President Roosevelt announced that there was no longer a military necessity for the exclusion of the Japanese aliens and Americans from the West Coast. Scholars have argued that the Supreme Court delayed handing down its decision until after President Roosevelt had won reelection in November and was ready to close the camps.

Years of Infamy

President Roosevelt declared that December 7, 1941, would be remembered as "a date which will live in infamy." Nisei Michi Weglyn paraphrased Roosevelt's words in the title of her book *Years of Infamy* (1976) to describe the incarceration of the Japanese Americans.

The assembly centers provided temporary housing for the evacuees while the camps in the interior were hastily being built. Many of the assembly centers were race tracks or fair grounds.

At the race tracks, families were assigned to renovated horse stalls, which still smelled of manure and hay. The partitions between the stalls did not reach the ceiling, so there was no privacy. Nisei Yoshiko Uchida described how the children changed their game of playing house from sitting around a table eating dinner to standing in line for food.

The ten concentration camps were all located in remote areas either in the desert or on swampland. Living conditions were minimally adequate. Tom Watanabe recalled when he and his family first arrived at Manzanar.

"They assigned us to a barracks with three other families. I mean, not families of the people that went up with us, but people I never met in my life. Four families in one room. No partition or nothing. The room was twenty by twenty. . . . All we had was room enough to walk by. You had the dust storm come through. You get half an inch of dust. You either get in bed and cover yourself with a sheet or just stand there and suffer. You couldn't even see three feet in front of you, and then by the time the dust storm was settled, you had at least half an inch of dust right on your sheet when you got under it. Used to come from underneath the floor. The floor used to have at least half an inch openings."

Watanabe's wife was pregnant when they arrived in Manzanar. She died after childbirth from internal bleeding. The twins she bore died within a day of their mother; Watanabe never saw his children, their birth certificates, or their death certificates. His tragic experience was one of many caused by the incarceration.

From the beginning, small numbers of inmates were allowed to leave the camps to work on farms or other menial labor in the interior of the country. College students were also allowed to leave to continue their education. The number of inmates who were granted leave was relatively small, however. The main obstacle to granting leave to more people was determining their loyalty.

Meanwhile, the U.S. army decided to create an all-Nisei combat team of about 5,000 men. WRA officials met with War Department officials to discuss recruitment details. In their discussions, the army officials stated that a questionnaire should be created to determine the Nisei's loyalty. The WRA agreed to the questionnaire, and decided to give it to all inmates over seventeen years old, regardless of sex or nationality. With the help of the questionnaire, the WRA hoped to speed up the relocation process.

As part of the recruiting effort, President Roosevelt made a public statement in January, 1943, praising the creation of an all-Nisei combat team:

"No loyal citizen of the United States should be denied the democratic right to exercise the responsibilities of citizenship, regardless of his ancestry. The principle on which this country was founded and by which it has been governed is that Americanism is a matter of the mind and the heart; Americanism is not, and never was, a matter of race or ancestry. A good

Following evacuation orders, this store was closed. On the day after Pearl Harbor, the owner, a University of California graduate of Japanese descent, had put up the sign proclaiming his allegiance to the United States. (Dorothea Lange/National Archives)

American is one who is loyal to this country and to our creed of liberty and democracy. Every loyal American citizen should be given the opportunity to serve the country wherever his skills will make the greatest contribution — whether it be in the ranks of the armed forces, war production, agriculture, government service, or other work essential to the war effort."

Given their confined state, many inmates must have questioned the President's sincerity. In February, 1943, the questionnaire was passed out to the camp residents. Two questions caused controversy and resulted in camp and family divisions. Question 27 asked whether one was willing to serve in the United States military, in combat. Question 28 asked the person to swear unqualified allegiance to the United States and give up any allegiance to the Japanese emperor. These two questions had been written particularly for the Nisei males of military age. Women, Issei, and older Nisei must have been puzzled by question 27. The content of question 28, however, was more disturbing. For the Issei, who were not allowed to become American citizens, it gave them a stateless status. For the Nisei, it assumed that the person filling out the questionnaire had an allegiance to the Japanese emperor. Eventually, question 28 was rewritten for Issei, asking whether they swore to abide by United States laws and not to take action against the United States.

About 75,000 inmates filled out the questionnaire; 6,700 said no to question 28, almost 2,000 qualified their answers and were thus determined disloyal, a few hundred did not reply, and more than 65,000 answered yes. The percentage of "no no" answers to the questionnaire varied greatly from camp to camp, depending on how close the camp was to the West Coast and how the camp administration handled the situation. At the Minidoka camp in Idaho, the camp director allowed public discussions of the questionnaire, and all grievances were addressed. Open discussion also was permitted prior to the arrival of the Army recruiters. As a result, Minidoka had the largest number of volunteers. In contrast, the Tule Lake camp in California was a disaster. Forty-two percent of the inmates answered "no" to the loyalty questions, and only 51 Nisei volunteered for the 442nd. The camp director used false threats of imprisonment and forced repatriation to try to get the Nisei to register. In February, 1943, thirty-five Nisei were arrested for refusing to register. Panic reigned as frightened evacuees tried to register but were hounded by angry, militant inmates, who supported the thirty-five imprisoned Nisei.

The 442nd Regimental Combat Team

Eventually the 442nd Regimental Combat Team would consist of 4,500 Nisei volunteers, with another 1,300 Nisei from the 100th Infantry Battalion of Hawaii. For many Nisei, it was a chance to prove their loyalty. While the 442nd Regimental Combat Team and the 100th Infantry Battalion were in training, Nisei were serving the army as translators, interpreters, and interrogators on the Pacific front of the war. These Nisei were graduates of the Military Intelligence Language Specialist School, which started in November, 1941. At first, classes were held in an abandoned airplane hangar at Crissey Field, near San Francisco, California. A total of 5,000 Nisei would fight in the Pacific. Because they were able to crack many of the secret codes of the Japanese army, they have been credited with shortening the war by two years and saving more than one million lives. The military kept these Nisei contributions secret for thirty years, at which time the documents relating to their wartime work were finally declassified.

The 442nd Regimental Combat Team and the 100th Infantry Battalion would become the most decorated unit in military history. The 100th Infantry Battalion became known as the Purple Heart Battalion. The Nisei soldiers would be at the front of seven campaigns against the Germans and Italians. Their casualty list, which includes both wounded and killed, numbered almost 9,500. When the war ended, parades and speeches welcomed the Nisei back to their homeland. President Harry Truman

recognized the true extent of their sacrifice in a speech at
Washington, D.C.: "You fought not only the enemy but you
fought prejudice, and you won. Keep up that fight and we'll
continue to win and make this great republic stand for just what
its Constitution says its stands for: the welfare of all the people all
the time."

Tule Lake and Heart Mountain

As a result of the questionnaire and pressure from Congress to
weed out the "disloyal," more than 18,000 evacuees were placed
in the Tule Lake camp by July, 1943. Tule Lake became a
maximum security segregated camp. Designed to house 15,000,
the camp squeezed in all those who had refused or failed to
answer or answered "no" to question 28 on the loyalty
questionnaire; who had applied for repatriation or expatriation to
Japan; whose loyalty was considered "questionable" by the camp
director; or who had been denied leave from the camp.

Of the 18,000, many of the 6,000 original Tule Lake inmates
had decided to stay in order to avoid being transferred again.
Half of the population was under eighteen. The conditions at Tule
Lake were worse than those in federal prisons. A riot, a strike,
and demonstrations eventually led to the military taking over Tule
Lake. A curfew was enforced, tear gas was used on crowds that
refused to disperse, arrests were made, schools were closed, and
work was reduced to a minimum. Those arrested were placed in
a stockade and completely isolated from the rest of the camp.
Relatives and friends were forbidden to see them for months.
There were rumors of beatings and interrogations. More than two
hundred inmates went on a hunger strike to protest the arrests
and camp conditions. After much outside protest from within the
United States and from Japan, the stockade was torn down in
August, 1944. It would be rebuilt a year later in the wake of the
renunciation problem.

At Heart Mountain, a group of Nisei formed the Fair Play
Committee in late 1943 to protest registration for the army.

Among them were Kiyoshi Okamoto, Paul Nakadate, Ben
Wakaye, Ken Yamagi, Frank Emi, Minoru Tamesa, and Sam
Horino. They were supported by James Omura, the editor of the
Japanese American newspaper *Rocky Shimpo*. The Fair Play
Committee believed that their rights as citizens should be restored
before they had to register for the draft. In one of their leaflets,
they argued "We would gladly sacrifice our lives to protect and
uphold the principles and ideals of our country as set forth in the
Constitution and the Bill of Rights ... but have we been given
such freedom, such liberty, such justice?" They also protested
the creation of a segregated unit. Sixty-three Nisei resisted the
draft at Heart Mountain and were arrested for violating the
Selective Service Act. They were tried and convicted in June,
1944, and sentenced to three years in prison. They would be
joined by another 22 from Heart Mountain and 44 from
Minidoka. The leaders of the Fair Play Committee were tried and
convicted for conspiracy to violate the Selective Service Act and
were sentenced to four years in prison. They appealed, and their
conviction was overturned in 1946.

6 Rebuilding the Community (1946-1966)

In Hawaii after the war, the Nisei became involved in politics through their labor unions. The International Longshoremen's and Warehousemen's Union (ILWU) created a political action committee (PAC) to raise money for political candidates who were committed to union demands. Through the PAC, the ILWU elected representatives to the territorial senate and was able to pass laws allowing agricultural workers to bargain collectively with the plantation owners.

In 1946, 28,000 plantation workers went on strike, shutting down 33 of the 34 plantations. After 79 days, the plantation owners gave in to the workers' demands for higher pay and a forty-hour work week.

This victory dramatically illustrated the importance of worker unity and the need to overcome racial barriers. The Nisei played an important role in integrating the Japanese workers with the Filipinos, Portuguese, Chinese, Hawaiians, and Puerto Ricans. Eighty percent of the Japanese working on the plantations were Nisei, and their ties to Japan were much weaker than that of their parents. They were eager to integrate the unions.

Returning veterans also played a large role in changing the politics in Hawaii. Veterans supported the Democratic party,

After the incarceration, many Japanese American businesses had to start all over again.
(Robert Brenner/PhotoEdit)

which consisted of Nisei, Chinese, and other minorities. In the 1954 local election, the Democratic party won control of the territorial Congress and many city and county offices. Nisei candidates won almost half of the Congressional seats.

Statehood for Hawaii

In March, 1959, Hawaii became a state. Attempts to become a state had failed in the past because those on the mainland were unable to accept the idea of a state that was predominantly nonwhite in population, particularly Japanese. During the war, Japanese Americans proved themselves both at home and abroad, and many of the more blatant displays of anti-Japanese feelings disappeared. In the first state election, Daniel Inouye, a Nisei veteran, was elected to the House of Representatives. Inouye had been part of the much-decorated 442nd battalion and had lost one arm in battle. Inouye became a senator in 1962. His House seat was filled by another Nisei veteran, Spark Matsunaga. In 1964, Hawaii was granted another House seat, which was won by Hawaii's first Nisei woman attorney, Patsy Takemoto Mink.

Thus, the Japanese Americans in Hawaii began making great strides politically and economically after World War II. The 1946 plantation strike broke the stranglehold of the plantation owners over the island's economy. As a result of the interracial unity of the plantation workers, a new generation of leaders led Hawaii toward statehood.

The Mainland Community

After the war, the mainland Japanese American community had to start over. Whereas most Americans had profited from the economic boom created by the war, Japanese Americans were behind barbed wire, earning at most sixteen dollars a week. Many had lost their land and businesses. It is estimated that the

Japanese lost approximately 370 million dollars in income and property as a result of their incarceration. In 1992 dollars, that amounts to more than two billion dollars. With the removal of some of the more blatant barriers in the 1950's and 1960's, however, Nisei were able to find jobs outside of their community in the areas in which they were trained. Those who had relocated to the Midwest found less discrimination than on the West Coast.

During the war, almost 30,000 Japanese Americans relocated to Chicago from the camps. Of those 30,000, half returned to the West Coast after the region was opened to them. Chicago was attractive to many Japanese Americans because there were jobs and the discrimination they experienced was minor if nonexistent when compared to that of the West Coast. Whereas the newspapers in California were blatantly anti-Japanese, four of the five Chicago daily papers supported the Japanese settlement.

Yet there were problems. Many Issei farmers had a difficult time adjusting to urban life and the menial jobs they were able to find. Many Issei could not speak or understand English well enough to communicate, which led to misunderstandings. Initially, Chicago employers and landlords were reluctant to hire or rent to Japanese. Many believed the propaganda and stereotypes they had heard or read during the war about Japanese. With pressure from city and community leaders, however, employers and landlords gave the new arrivals a chance and were pleasantly surprised to find ideal workers and tenants.

One of the most unusual problems encountered by the Japanese American community in Chicago concerned the use of cemeteries. Of the twenty-six cemeteries in Chicago in 1947, only one would bury Japanese. After much pressure from the city government and the Chicago press, a few more cemeteries agreed to allow Japanese to be buried in their graveyards.

After the camps closed, 54,127 Issei and Nisei returned to the West Coast. On the West Coast, they received a mixed welcome. The bravery of the 442nd Combat Team and the 100th Battalion preceded them in some places, and neighbors helped them start over. There were a number of cases of vandalism, however. In

Ikebana, or flower arranging, is one of the traditional Japanese arts practiced by many Japanese Americans. (Kimberly Dawson)

Seattle, Washington, Japanese American homes were defaced. In Placer Country, California, there was an attempt to blow up a Japanese American packing shed.

A Postwar Agenda

In February, 1946, the JACL had its first postwar national convention. President Saburo Kido proposed that the JACL fight legalized discrimination in three areas: naturalization rights for the Issei, repayment from the federal government for losses suffered from the evacuation and incarceration, and removal of the racist nature of immigration laws. Mike Masaoka was sent to Washington, D.C., to present the JACL's program to Congress.

The JACL's national agenda took second place to events happening in California. In early 1945, when the state government became aware that the Japanese soon would be returning to their homes, lawmakers gave $200,000 to the California Justice Department to enforce the Alien Land Law and confiscate Japanese-held lands, even land that was in the name of American-born children. Defendants had two choices: They could fight the government or pay the state half the land's appraised value. By late 1946, more than sixty cases were filed against the Japanese in California. Although most families made the payment, since they knew that otherwise they definitely would lose their land, a few chose to fight.

One landowner who refused to pay was Fred Oyama. Oyama was a Nisei whose parents had bought eight acres of farmland in their son's name. Oyama's father had been named legal guardian of the land. Whenever Oyama's father conducted business on behalf of his son's property, he went to court for approval. In 1944, while the Oyamas were in a concentration camp, the state Justice Department filed a suit against the Oyamas, charging that they had violated the Alien Land Law. On November 5, 1946, the California Supreme Court ruled against the Oyamas, who then appealed to the U.S. Supreme Court. Five days after the state Supreme Court ruling, California voters defeated a proposition that would have the alien land laws part of the state constitution. The JACL used newspapers, pamphlets, and public speeches to persuade voters that this proposition was wrong. Despite the California Supreme Court ruling and the powerful, financial support of those in favor of the proposition, the voters sided with the JACL and the immigrant communities 1,143,780 to 797,067.

Fresh from this victory, the JACL threw its support behind the Oyamas' case at the U.S. Supreme Court. In January, 1948, the United States Supreme Court overturned the lower courts' rulings, stating that the state's alien land laws violated Fred Oyama's rights as an American citizen on the basis of his ethnic origin. Thus, one aspect of the alien land law was invalidated, and the cases against Japanese American landowners were dropped. In 1952, the California Supreme Court ruled that state laws could not prevent aliens ineligible for citizenship from owning land. The death blow to the alien land laws came in 1956. That year, the JACL placed Proposition 13 on the California ballot, which provided for the repeal of the alien land laws. The proposition passed by a two-to-one margin, with more than two million people voting in favor.

While the Japanese Americans won victories in California, Mike Masaoka talked to legislators in Washington about the JACL and its national goals. The JACL's first victory in Congress came in July, 1947, with the passage of the Soldier Brides Act. This law made it possible for American soldiers who married Japanese women to bring them to the United States. Because of the 1924 Immigration Act, the couples would not have been allowed to enter the country. The Soldier Brides Act was the first hole in the fabric of the 1924 Immigration Act. In October, 1947, President Harry S Truman's Committee on Civil Rights released a report that showed a further breakdown of racial barriers. In its discussion of Japanese Americans, the report recommended that laws be passed allowing Japanese to file claims for lost property as a result of the evacuation and to become naturalized citizens. The report also recommended that states repeal discriminatory laws. In June, 1948, a law was passed offering citizenship to all aliens, regardless of their race, who had served in the American military during World Wars I and II. Like the Soldier Brides Act, this law chipped away at the 1924 Immigration Act.

About a month later, Congress passed the Evacuation Claims Act. Evacuees were given until January 3, 1950, to file claims for material losses. More than 23,000 claims were filed, totaling almost 132 million dollars. The Justice Department was put in charge of the program. Instead of looking at the program as a way to repay the evacuees for their losses, however, department officials felt it necessary to challenge each claim. As a result, the department spent an average of $1,400 to investigate a claim that it determined was worth $450. Congress took a hard look at the program and ordered that claimants could be paid three-fourths of their claim or $2,500, whichever was less. The last claim was settled in 1965; a total of $38 million was paid.

The JACL's fight to win naturalization rights for the Issei became entangled in the anti-Communist atmosphere of the 1950s. Although lobbyist Masaoka would have preferred to have a bill passed that dealt solely with removing race as a criteria for naturalization, he realized that he needed support from both conservative and liberal legislators to get what he wanted. In 1949, Congressman Walter Judd introduced a bill that would remove racial considerations from immigration and naturalization laws. In the process of getting it passed through the House and Senate, security measures were added to the bill to prevent Communists from entering the country or government. These measures seriously violated some basic human rights. As a result, President Truman vetoed the bill.

The JACL through Masaoka decided to support overriding the veto, despite the problems with the bill. Masaoka believed that passing the bill would not only give aliens the right to naturalization but also would prevent passage of the Internal Security Act, which had more severe security measures and was in process at Congress. The attempt to override the veto was unsuccessful. The Internal Security Act was passed in 1950 despite Truman's veto.

Calligraphy is another traditional Japanese art. (Michael Newman/PhotoEdit)

Immigration Policy

Meanwhile, Masaoka continued his efforts on the naturalization issue. In 1952, the Walter-McCarran Act was passed by Congress; it provided for a minimal immigration quota and eliminated race as an obstacle to naturalization. It also had more internal security measures. Although President Truman approved of the naturalization and immigration parts of the act, he was unable to approve of the bill because of security measures. Congress overrode Truman's veto again, however. For the JACL, passage of the bill was an emotional triumph. It was a chance for the Nisei to express their gratitude to their parents for the hard work, dedication, and sacrifices. The Issei responded eagerly. By 1965, about 46,000 Issei had become naturalized citizens.

While the McCarran-Walter Act did allow those Asians in the United States to become citizens, it placed extremely restrictive quotas on further Asian immigration. In 1964, Congress responded to the Civil Rights Movement by outlawing racial discrimination. In 1965, it passed a new Immigration Act, which abolished national origins as a criteria for immigration. Instead it provided for the annual admission of 170,000 immigrants from the Eastern Hemisphere and 120,000 from the Western Hemisphere, not including family members of American citizens.

As a result of the 1965 Immigration Act, a new wave of Asians arrived in the United States. Of these, only 4,000 came from Japan annually. Between 1965 and 1984, less than 100,000 Japanese immigrated to the United States. In large part, the low immigration numbers are a result of Japan's postwar economic success. In order to achieve the level of industrialization that it did, Japan needed labor and therefore discouraged emigration. Because so few Japanese immigrated, the Japanese population in the United States became proportionately more Americanized.

7 Redress and Reparations (1967-1991)

In 1967, the first academic conference on the incarceration was held at the University of California at Los Angeles. At the time, the main discussion concerned whether or not it could happen again. Not all members of the Japanese American community were happy with the idea of the conference. They believed that such discussion would lead only to a renewal of anti-Japanese hostility. Others, however, began talking about getting redress for their imprisonment.

At the 1970 JACL conference in Chicago, Edison Uno introduced a resolution to make redress the JACL's primary issue. Uno pushed for redress at the next two JACL conventions in 1972 and in 1974; in 1974 his resolution was passed. In spite of the resolution being passed, however, little was accomplished. Uno's activist stance was not in favor with the JACL leadership, who failed to act on the resolutions. At the next convention in 1976, the JACL reaffirmed its commitment to redress and decided that monetary payment would be one of the essential parts of the redress movement.

That same year, one of the most important books in Japanese American history was published. In *Years of Infamy*, Michi Weglyn brought to light the Munson report and the fact that the

military knew of Munson's findings about the overwhelming
loyalty of the Japanese community. Weglyn concluded from her
research that "under the guise of an emergency and pretended
threats to the national security, the citizenry was denied the
known facts, public opinion skillfully manipulated, and a cruel
and massive governmental hoax enacted." Weglyn also unearthed
WRA reports that documented the use of informants in the
camps, the Tule Lake riots, and the renunciation program.
Weglyn's book crushed the government's use of military necessity
to defend the evacuation and incarceration.

A Plan for Redress

In late 1977, Uno died, and Clifford Uyeda took over the fight
for redress. Uyeda had been involved with a number of civil
rights activities, including getting a presidential pardon for Iva
Toguri, who had been incorrectly branded and imprisoned as
"Tokyo Rose." In early 1978, Uyeda brought together
representatives from each of the eight JACL districts to come up
with a plan for redress to present at the next JACL convention
that summer. In that convention, Uyeda was elected president of
the JACL; he appointed John Tateishi head of the redress
committee. With Uyeda, Tateishi came up with two goals for the
next two years: to educate the public about the redress movement
and to get legislation drafted and introduced into Congress.

After talking with Japanese American members of Congress,
Tateishi's National Committee for Redress met in San Francisco
in early March, 1979. The committee rejected filing a law suit
against the government. After two days, they followed the advice
of the Japanese American legislators. Given the political climate,
they decided that the best route would be to seek legislation to
create a fact-finding commission, which would investigate the
incarceration.

In August, 1979, Senators Daniel Inouye, Spark Matsunaga,
Sam Hayakawa, and Ted Stevens introduced the JACL bill to

create an investigative commission and put aside $1.5 billion to cover the costs of the commission. Six weeks later, the same bill was introduced in the House by Representative James Wright, Norman Mineta, and Bob Matsui, among others. In November of the same year, Representative Mike Lowry introduced a bill on behalf of the NCJAR, which called for a total of three billion dollars to be paid to former camp inmates.

Testimony from the Incarceration

In May, 1980, the Senate passed the JACL bill; and the House of Representatives passed it in July, 1980. Ten days after the House passed the bill, President Jimmy Carter formed the Commission on Wartime Relocation and Internment of Civilians (CWRIC). The CWRIC held hearings in several major cities across the country from July to December, 1981. Approximately 750 people testified of their wartime experiences, many of them for the first time. For many Nisei, it was very difficult to talk about what they had gone through.

The hearings brought the Japanese American community together. Psychologically, the act of giving testimony, though painful, began the healing process that the Japanese American community had denied itself for forty years. Moreover, testifying gave these people a chance to contribute to righting a wrong, to fight for civil rights.

As a result of the testimony, the CWRIC put together their findings in the report entitled *Personal Justice Denied*, which was published in February, 1983. The CWRIC found that the incarceration of the Japanese was unjustified by military necessity and was the result of "race prejudice, war hysteria and a failure of political leadership. . . . A grave injustice was done to American citizens and resident aliens of Japanese ancestry who, without individual review or any probative evidence against them, were excluded, removed and detained by the United States during World War II."

Close family ties sustained Japanese Americans through times of adversity. (Felicia Martinez/PhotoEdit)

In June, 1983, the CWRIC followed up the report with five recommendations. First, it called for a joint congressional resolution that acknowledged and apologized for the injustice suffered by the Japanese Americans during World War II. Second, the CWRIC recommended a presidential pardon for those convicted of violating the evacuation and incarceration orders. Third, it urged Congress to order government offices to handle liberally claims by Japanese Americans who had lost their status and benefits as a result of discrimination. For example, Japanese American soldiers who were discharged from the army at the beginning of the war lost veteran status and benefits. Fourth, the CWRIC recommended that Congress put aside funds to establish a foundation which would sponsor education and research on the causes and context of this and similar events in order to teach the public. Finally, the CWRIC suggested that each survivor of the camps be paid $20,000 as a token compensation for the loss of civil rights they experienced during the war. At an estimated 60,000 survivors, the total payment would amount to $1.2 billion.

The Civil Liberties Act of 1988

In September, 1987, the House of Representatives passed a bill that wrote into law all five of the commission's recommendations. In April, 1988, the Senate passed a similar bill. After ironing out the differences between the two bills, the Senate passed the revised version in late July, and the House passed it in early August. The fact that 1988 was an election year changed the minds of a number of politicians, including President Ronald Reagan. Just before the House vote, President Reagan reversed his position on the redress and endorsed the bill. On August 10, 1988, President Reagan signed the bill into law, which became known as the Civil Liberties Act of 1988.

Actual payment became a victim of budget battles in Congress. Survivors would have to wait another two years after the signing ceremony before funds were put aside and the first payments made on October 10, 1990. For those who died after August 10, 1988, their heirs would receive the $20,000. Those who died before August 10 received nothing.

Legal Resolution

At around the same time as the CWRIC's hearings, a lawyer named Peter Irons began researching the wartime Supreme Court cases brought against the U.S. by Hirabayashi, Korematsu, and Yasui. Irons was interested in the strategies and tactics used by the forty lawyers involved in the cases. He was particularly interested in how wartime affected justice. During his research, Irons uncovered evidence that the government lawyers knew that the most important military document presented to the Supreme Court contained false information. Furthermore, the War Department had altered or destroyed documents that would have contradicted its stand that the incarceration of Japanese Americans was a military necessity.

Irons contacted the three men individually to discuss what he had found. "They did me a great wrong," said Korematsu, after reading through the documents Irons presented. Along with Hirabayashi and Yasui, Korematsu agreed to try to clear their convictions. All three filed for a reversal of their convictions in January, 1983. Arguing that their original trials were tainted by the use of false information, they petitioned for a writ of error *coram nobis*. At the time, all three were in their mid-sixties. At a press conference in San Francisco after Korematsu filed his petition, each of the three spoke. "I was born and schooled in Oakland," said Korematsu. "I'm just like any other American." Hirabayashi said he had defied the curfew and evacuation orders because "If I gave in to this, it would cause me to change my ideals, my beliefs, my whole philosophy of life. I knew I'd be accused of disloyalty, but I couldn't sit back and passively endorse the orders." Yasui spoke of the nine months he had spent

in solitary confinement and showed a copy of the Constitution
that his father had given him as a child.

One of the first problems that Korematsu's lawyers confronted
resulted from the CWRIC's recommendations. The CWRIC had
recommended that the President pardon those convicted of
violating any of the orders associated with evacuation and
internment. The government never officially offered a pardon,
however, and the three petitioners decided they would have
refused to accept the pardon had it been offered. Instead, the
government's lawyer, Victor Stone, used the possibility of a
pardon as a delaying tactic. In the initial hearing, Stone tried to
get Korematsu's case dismissed by refusing to defend the original
conviction. In November, 1983, having listened to lawyers from
both sides, the Judge Marilyn Patel granted Korematsu's petition
and vacated his conviction. In her opinion, Patel referred to
General DeWitt's views as "infected with racism."

In January, 1984, the Judge Belloni heard the first arguments in
Yasui's case. Again, the government's lawyer, Stone, asked that
the case be dismissed and Yasui's conviction be vacated. Ten days
later, Belloni ruled in favor of the government, vacating Yasui's
conviction but refusing to look into the acts of government
misconduct charged by Yasui. "I decline to make such findings
forty years after the events took place. … Courts should not
engage in that kind of activity." Yasui appealed the decision and
soon found his case entangled in technicalities. In November,
1986, Yasui died. Yasui's family continued to appeal the decision.
In 1987, the Supreme Court refused to consider the posthumous
petition on the grounds that it was moot.

Hirabayashi's was the last of the three cases to be heard. Judge
Donald Voorhees heard the first arguments on the petition in
May, 1984. Again, attorney Stone tried to get the case dismissed.
Unlike Belloni, Voorhees refused to dismiss Hirabayashi's
petition. "What he really is seeking now is vindication of his
honor, and I feel that he has that right." Voorhees then set a date
of June 17, 1985, for the next hearing. Although Stone tried to
delay the hearing, Voorhees refused. Although the majority of

the case consisted of presentation of documents, some of the
testimony of witnesses provided excitement for the packed
courtroom. One of the most dramatic confrontations was the
cross-examination of the government's star witness, David
Lowman. Lowman was formerly employed by the National
Security Agency. According to Lowman's research, there was
proof that Japanese Americans had spied for Japan. During cross-
examination, however, it was revealed that the source for the
espionage claims was the *Los Angeles Times*. Lowman was
forced to admit that his definition of intelligence sources included
newspapers, which completely destroyed his credibility.

On February 10, 1986, Judge Voorhees issued his opinion on
the Hirabayashi case. Voorhees reversed the conviction of
Hirabayashi's violation of the evacuation order but not of the
curfew order, which he called a "relatively mild" burden.
Hirabayashi and the government both appealed Voorhees' ruling:
Hirabayashi wanted reversal of the curfew conviction and the
government wanted to reinstate the evacuation conviction. In the
appeals court, the three judges ruled in favor of Hirabayashi and
returned the case to Voorhees court with orders to reverse both
convictions. On January 12, 1988, Judge Voorhees erased both
convictions and concluded: "It is now conceded by almost
everyone that the internment of Japanese Americans during
World War II was a tragic mistake for which American society as
a whole must accept responsibility. If, in the future, this country
should find itself in a comparable national emergency, the
sacrifices made by Gordon Hirabayashi, Fred Korematsu, and
Minoru Yasui may, it is hoped, stay the hand of government
again tempted to imprison a defenseless minority without trial
and for no offense."

8 The Model Minority

The Japanese Americans and other Asian Americans are being held up to other minorities as a model minority. Politicians point to the success and achievement of Asian Americans; they applaud their hard work and thrift. Such a label may seem positive, but it is a stereotype; and, like any stereotype, it leads to discrimination and misunderstanding. What Japanese Americans have accomplished is in large part due to unique cultural values, such as obligation to one's family and community. Applying such a label denies the unique experience of the Japanese Americans and the fact that their response was neither standard nor easily imitated. It also denies the fact that the Japanese American community has problems that need to be addressed and solved and that the community needs help from the government to solve them.

In addition, being labeled a model minority washes over the fact that Asian Americans are still not being treated equally. When comparing incomes between Asian American and Caucasian American families, politicians have applauded the Asians for being above the total American average. Such comparisons do not take into account the fact that Japanese Americans are concentrated in California and Hawaii, which have higher costs of living than the total American average. Moreover, Japanese American families on average have more persons working than Caucasian American families: in 1980,

As a result of their outstanding success, Japanese Americans and other Asian Americans have been called "the model minority," a positive but misleading stereotype. (PhotoEdit)

Caucasian American families in California had 1.6 workers per family, and Japanese American families had 2.1. Finally, for their level of education, Japanese American workers have lower incomes than Caucasian Americans.

Asian Americans continue to face discrimination in school and at their jobs. At many prestigious universities, Asian Americans are overrepresented in relation to their numbers in the overall population. At Harvard University, for example, the freshman class in the late 1980's was about 20 percent Asian; according to the 1990 census, Asians represent less than 3 percent of the total population. Yet university officials at Harvard have stated that Asians have a lower admission rate than whites, because they do less well in athletics and fewer of them have alumni as parents. Because of their high representation at universities such as the University of California at Los Angeles, anti-Asian hostility has increased. Asian students are stereotyped as "nerds" who ruin grade curves and have no social life. Anti-Asian graffiti has appeared on university walls, such as "Stop the Yellow Hordes" and "U.C.L.A. stands for University of Caucasians Living among Asians."

At work, Japanese Americans and other Asian American minorities talk about the glass ceiling. Although they have been able to find jobs as professionals, few are promoted to managerial or supervisory positions. According to Ron Takaki in *Strangers from a Different Shore*, of the 29,000 officers and directors of the one thousand largest companies in the United States, less than 150 are Asian American. Whereas Japanese Americans blame their lack of promotion on not having the connections that their white counterparts have, white managers argue that as a whole, Asian Americans are not aggressive or articulate enough to be good leaders. The truth may be a combination of both. In both cases, the stereotype of the model minority, the quiet, unassuming, diligent, yet unimaginative worker is a part of the problem.

Japan-Bashing

In addition to the model minority stereotype, the Japanese Americans face the return of an older stereotype. The trade imbalance between Japan and the United States has chilled relations between the two countries. Looking for a scapegoat during economic hard times, the American government has blamed Japan. The stereotype of the cunning, inscrutable Oriental has returned to haunt the Japanese, and, as a result, Japanese Americans. Americans have had difficulty distinguishing between Japanese and Japanese Americans in the past. It appears that in the present atmosphere of Japan bashing, the public has learned very little. The JACL has received a record number of hate letters in 1991, as trade talks between Japan and the United States stalled and more and more Americans lost their jobs. In 1982, a Chinese American named Vincent Chin was murdered by two white autoworkers, who thought he was Japanese. "Buy American" has been translated into "Boycott Japanese."

Overcoming Stereotypes

Going beyond the stereotypes, seeing the depth, and accepting the complex nature of each human being is difficult yet essential. Stereotypes dehumanize those who are labeled and those who assign the labels. The label model minority may seem harmless, but it is not. It puts up barriers to a true understanding of those who are different. It destroys the natural curiosity that humans have to explore and learn about their surroundings.

Japanese Americans have worked hard to overcome the stereotypes attached to them. For the Sansei, the 1960's and 1970's gave them a chance to become more vocal and assertive about their ethnic identity. Rather than try to blend in and

A rice importer; economic tensions have provoked Japan-bashing, threatening Japanese Americans as well. (PhotoEdit)

assimilate, many Sansei were swept up in the pro-ethnic movement. They joined in anti-Vietnam protests. At universities, they joined other Asian Americans and pushed for and won the establishment of Asian American studies programs. They began to question their parents about the wartime years, about the camps. The Sansei could not understand their parents' silence and reluctance to talk about the injustice they had experienced.

The redress movement that began in the 1970's and continued through the 1980's was a product of the explosion of ethnic consciousness during the 1960's and 1970's. In addition to the redress issue, Japanese Americans have become committed to educating themselves and others about the Japanese American experience. The National Japanese American Historical Society, the Japanese American National Museum, and the Japanese American Library were all developed in the 1980's.

The Japanese American National Museum was founded in 1985 as a private, nonprofit institution. Its purpose is to educate Americans about the experience of Japanese Americans. The museum is housed in a renovated Buddhist temple in Little Tokyo in Los Angeles, California. Those involved with the museum worked toward the opening day in late April, 1992 with excitement. The museum is the first in the United States to focus solely on Japanese Americans. Many Japanese Americans involved with the museum emphasize the importance of telling their own story, rather than having it interpreted and presented by others. No matter how hard they try, non-Japanese Americans will be describing the Japanese American experience as outsiders. By establishing the museum, Japanese Americans have taken responsibility for their past; the history they write will be their own.

9 Some Who Made a Difference

Many Japanese Americans have participated in the struggle for equality. The contributions of ordinary men and women are the lifeblood of the community.

At the same time, certain individuals stand out for their role in the struggle against racism and discrimination. Chapter 5, for example, highlighted the landmark cases of Gordon Hirabayashi, Fred Korematsu, and Minoru Yasui, who challenged the harshly unfair treatment of Japanese Americans during World War II.

This chapter briefly considers the contributions of several outstanding Japanese Americans. Their achievements are representative of many others from the Japanese American community; many of them testify not only to individual determination but also to the importance of collective action: people working together for the good of the community.

Kyutaro Abiko

Abiko was one of the most influential Issei immigrant leaders on the mainland. Arriving as a student-laborer in San Francisco in 1885, he studied English and worked in menial jobs. In 1899, he started what would become the most read Japanese language newspaper, *Nichibei Shimbun* (Japanese American news). In 1902, he cofounded the biggest labor contracting company in

California, the Japanese American Industrial Corporation of San Francisco. Abiko was a major advocate of permanent settlement; according to Yuji Ichioka in *The Issei*, Abiko "more than anyone else, influenced many Issei to sink their roots in American soil." He believed that permanent settlement was the only way to end hostility against Japanese, and used both his standing in the community and his own money to help those who decided to make the United States their home.

George Ryochi Ariyoshi

Ariyoshi was the first Japanese-American state governor. Born in Honolulu in March, 1926, he fought with the 100th Infantry Battalion during World War II. After his return to the United States, he went to law school at the University of Michigan. He was elected as territorial representative of Hawaii from 1954 to 1958, after which he won a seat in the state House of Representatives. In 1970, he became lieutenant governor of Hawaii. Ariyoshi was elected governor in 1974 and served three consecutive terms until 1986.

William Hohri

Hohri was chair of the National Council for Japanese American Redress (NCJAR), which was formed in 1979. Hohri and the NCJAR were dissatisfied with the JACL decision to advocate a fact-finding commission. The NCJAR introduced a redress bill into Congress during the same session that the JACL introduced its redress bill. The NCJAR asked for three billion dollars total; the JACL asked for 1.5 billion dollars. The JACL bill was adopted. The NCJAR filed a class action suit against the government in March, 1983, demanding payment to all 120,000 victims of the incarceration. The suit was dismissed. Hohri and the NCJAR represented an alternative voice to the JACL in the fight for redress and reparations.

Daniel Inouye

Born in Hawaii in September, 1924, Inouye fought in World
War II in the 442nd Regimental Combat Team and lost an arm.
His heroism earned him a Distinguished Service Cross. Because
of his injury, Inouye decided to pursue law as a career rather than
medicine when he returned to the United States in 1947. In 1959,
he became the first Japanese American congressman; in 1963, he
became the first Japanese American senator. Inouye was the
keynote speaker at the 1968 Democratic Convention. He sat on
the Senate Watergate Committee and chaired the Iran-Contra
Affair Committee. Inouye was one of several congressmen who
fought for redress for the Japanese Americans.

Frederick Kinzaburo Makino

Makino was one of the main Hawaiian immigrant leaders, who
became prominent during the sugar strike of 1909. He became
one of the leaders of the Higher Wage Association, which
represented Japanese plantation workers in their struggle for
better pay and living conditions. Born in 1877, Makino was the
son of an Englishman and Japanese woman. He arrived in Hawaii
in 1899 and found a job as a clerk one of the plantations. In 1901,
he opened a drugstore in Honolulu. After the 1909 strike,
Makino created a newspaper called the *Hawaii Hochi*, in which
he urged the Japanese workers to fight for their rights. From
protesting assembly line marriages to advocating naturalization
rights for Issei to taking the territorial government to court over
the anti-Japanese language school legislation, Makino confronted
the government and the plantation owners on behalf of the
Japanese workers.

Daniel Inouye. (Daniel Inouye)

Spark Masayuki Matsunaga

Born in 1916 in Kauai, Matsunaga was a member of the 442nd Regimental Combat Team and the 100th Battalion. After returning to the United States, he received a law degree from Harvard University. After graduation, he held a number of government posts with the Truman administration. Matsunaga replaced Daniel Inouye in the House of Representatives when the latter was elected to the Senate in 1963. Reelected four times as a House Representative, Matsunaga also served in the Senate from 1976 to 1988.

Dale Minami

Minami was born in Los Angeles in 1946. He received a law degree from University of California's School of Law. He founded the Asian American Law Caucus and the Asian Pacific Bar of California. Minami was an active member of the Bay Area Attorneys for Redress (BAAR), which consisted of twenty lawyers and legal aides. BAAR submitted a document to the Commission on Wartime Relocation and Internment of Civilians which stated that the internment was unconstitutional. Minami served as lead counsel in reopening Fred Korematsu's case, which resulted in removing Korematsu's forty-year old conviction.

Patsy Takemoto Mink

Born in Maui, Hawaii, in 1947, Mink was the first Nisei woman lawyer in Hawaii. She received her law degree from University of Chicago in 1951. Mink was elected to the House of Representatives in 1964. President Jimmy Carter appointed her Assistant Secretary of State for Oceans and International Environment and Scientific Affairs. In 1990, she was reelected to the House of Representatives.

Janice Mirikitani

Mirikitani's poetry has paralleled her activism in civil rights and, in particular, the redress movement. Her collection *Shedding Silence: Poetry and Prose* (1987) looks at the incarceration and its effects on later generations. One of her poems, "Prisons of Silence," was performed by the Asian American Dance Collective in 1983. The poem describes how the silence of the Issei and Nisei about the incarceration stifled and crippled the community and the individual. "I rebuilt my life/like a wall, unquestioning./Obeyed their laws . . . their laws." It then ends with the healing effects of the redress movement and the chance to testify at the commission hearings. "We give testimony./Our noise is dangerous./We beat our hands/like wings healed./We soar/from these walls of silence."

Takie Okumura

Born in Japan in 1865, Okumura was one of the main Hawaiian immigrant leaders. His views were similar to Kyutaro Abiko's and rivaled those of Frederick Kinzaburo Makino. Okumura was converted to Christianity at age 23. He arrived in Honolulu in 1894, shortly after being ordained as a minister. He founded Makiki Church in 1904. Okumura wanted to build a stable, moral Japanese community. He believed in the Americanization of the Japanese and fought crime, gambling, and prostitution in the Japanese community. Although he founded one of the first Japanese language schools, Okumura later became one of its critics during the language school controversy in the 1920's.

Michi Weglyn

Born in 1929 in Brentwood, California, Weglyn spent World War II in the Gila concentration camp in Arizona, where she contracted tuberculosis. After her recovery and after the war, she worked as a costume designer for a television show. With the help of researchers Aiko Yoshinaga Herzig, Herzig's husband, and Yuri Kochiyama, Weglyn uncovered the Munson report about the overwhelming loyalty of the Japanese American population, which had been buried by the military. The publication of *Years of Infamy* in 1976 and the documents it uncovered led to the creation of the Commission on Wartime Relocation and Internment of Civilians and to the reopening of the cases of Hirabayashi, Korematsu, and Yasui. Her book is considered by some to be the one Asian American book to change Asian American history.

10 Time Line

1853	Two hundred years of Japan's self-imposed isolation from the world are ended.
1868	Pro-Western and industry leaders take over the Japanese government and put the emperor back on the throne.
	About 150 Japanese laborers arrive in Hawaii to work on the plantations. The venture fails, and Japan bans all further emigration.
1871	Japan and Hawaii sign a friendship treaty.
1873	The Japanese government enacts a military draft.
1876	United States and Hawaii sign a Reciprocity Treaty.
1882	United States passes the Chinese Exclusion Law.
1885	Japan lifts its ban on emigration and works out an agreement with Hawaii to send plantation laborers.
1885-1894	29,000 Japanese laborers arrive in Hawaii.
1886	Chinese are no longer allowed to immigrate to Hawaii.
1894-1908	125,000 Japanese immigrate to Hawaii under agreements between the Hawaiian kingdom and private Japanese companies. Another 17,000 arrive independently.
1898	Hawaii and the Philippines become U.S. territories.
1900	The United States passes the Organic Act. Japanese laborers begin immigrating to the mainland.
1902	The Chinese Exclusion Act is extended for ten more years.
1903	1,500 Japanese and Mexican farm workers strike in Oxnard, California.
1904	The Chinese Exclusion Act is extended indefinitely. Japanese laborers in Hawaii organize their first strike.
1905	The San Francisco School Board tries to segregate Japanese schoolchildren in Oriental schools. President Roosevelt convinces them not to segregate.
	The Asiatic Exclusion League is formed in San Francisco. California law is amended to prohibit marriages between whites and Asians.

1907	Japan and the United States sign the Gentlemen's Agreement. President Roosevelt signs Executive Order 589, which prevents Japanese with passports for Hawaii, Mexico, or Canada from entering the continental U.S.
1908	The Issei form the Japanese Association of America.
1909	7,000 Japanese plantation workers strike for four months on the island of Oahu.
1910-1920	More than 20,000 Japanese women arrive on the West Coast as picture brides.
1913	California passes the first alien land law.
1917	Arizona passes an alien land law.
1919	Japanese laborers in Hawaii form the Federation of Japanese Labor.
1920	10,000 Japanese and Filipino plantation workers go on strike. Japan agrees to stop issuing passports to picture brides. California amends its alien land law, closing many of the loopholes used by Issei.
1921	Washington and Louisiana pass alien land laws.
1922	The Supreme Court rules in *Takao Ozawa v. U.S.* that Japanese are ineligible for citizenship. New Mexico passes an alien land law. United States passes the Cable Act.
1923	Idaho, Montana, and Oregon pass alien land laws. Various cases uphold the constitutionality of Washington's and California's alien land laws.
1924	The United States passes the Immigration Act.
1930	Nisei form the Japanese American Citizens League.
1931	The Cable Act is amended to give naturalization rights to American women who have lost their citizenship by marrying aliens ineligible for citizenship.
12/7/1941	Japan bombs Pearl Harbor. Martial law is declared in Hawaii.
12/8/1941	The United States declares war on Japan. The government activates Sand Island Detention Camp in Hawaii to house detainees.
12/29/1941	All enemy aliens living in California, Oregon, Washington, Montana, Idaho, Utah, and Nevada are ordered to turn in all shortwave radios, cameras, binoculars, and weapons.
Jan-Feb, 1942	Politicians, business organizations, and groups such as the Native Sons of the Golden West publicly advocate the removal of all Japanese and Japanese Americans.
1/5/1942	All Japanese Americans registered with the selective service are classified in the same category as enemy aliens. Many Japanese

	Americans in the military are discharged or demoted to menial labor.
1/28/1942	All state employees of Japanese ancestry are dismissed from their jobs.
2/19/1942	President Franklin Roosevelt signs Executive Order 9066.
2/20/1942	Secretary of War Henry Stimson puts General John DeWitt in charge of enforcing Executive Order 9066.
3/2/1942	DeWitt declares that Washington, Oregon, California, and parts of Arizona are military areas 1 and 2. The proclamation also states that German, Italian, and Japanese aliens and any person of Japanese ancestry may be excluded from these two areas.
3/6/1942	DeWitt declares that Idaho, Montana, Nevada, and Utah are military areas 3 through 6.
3/18/1942	President Roosevelt issues Executive Order 9102, which creates the War Relocation Authority.
3/21/1942	Congress passes Public Law 503, which provides punishment for those who disobey any orders to leave or enter the military areas.
3/23/1942	DeWitt issues the first exclusion order.
6/7/1942	DeWitt announces that 100,000 persons of Japanese ancestry have been evacuated from military area 1.
6/12/1942	Minoru Yasui's trial begins. He is convicted.
7/9/1942	Evacuation of all persons of Japanese ancestry from military area 2 begins.
8/7/1942	DeWitt announces that 110,000 persons of Japanese ancestry have been evacuated from military areas 1 and 2 and that the evacuation is complete.
9/8/1942	Fred Korematsu's trial begins. He is convicted.
10/20/1942	Gordon Hirabayashi's trial begins. He is convicted.
10/30/1942	The WRA announces that the last assembly center has been closed down and that all evacuees have been transferred to the 10 relocation centers.
12/6/1942	Violence breaks out at the Manzanar Relocation Center after evacuees are arrested for beating another evacuee. Military police fire into the crowd, killing two and wounding ten evacuees.
1/28/1943	Nisei are allowed to volunteer for military service.
2/3/1943	The controversial loyalty questionnaire is handed out to all evacuees more than 17 years old. The 442nd Regimental Combat Team is activated. It consists of the 100th Battalion from Hawaii and volunteers from the mainland.
Apr, 1944	An Issei is shot and killed by military police at Topaz Relocation Center when he gets too close to the outer camp fence.

6/12/1943	The Supreme Court upholds Hirabayashi's conviction and sends Yasui's case back to the lower courts for resentencing based on the Hirabayashi case.
7/9/1943	The judge in Mitsuye Endo's case, which challenged the exclusion orders, dismisses her case.
7/31/1943	Tule Lake Relocation Center becomes a segregation camp for "disloyal" evacuees.
11/1/1943	The military takes control of Tule Lake after mass demonstrations by inmates.
1/14/1944	The WRA resumes control of Tule Lake from the military.
1/20/1944	Japanese Americans become eligible for the draft.
6/30/1944	Jerome Relocation Center is closed. The remaining evacuees are transferred to other camps.
7/18/1944	Sixty-three men from Heart Mountain Relocation Center are convicted of resisting the draft.
Oct, 1944	The 442nd's extraordinary courage earns the spotlight when the team rescues the "Lost Battalion."
12/17/1944	General Henry Pratt, who replaced DeWitt, proclaims that evacuees can return to their homes.
12/18/1944	The Supreme Court upholds Korematsu's conviction and rules in Endo's case that the government cannot detain loyal citizens.
1944-1945	About 5,700 evacuees apply to renounce their American citizenship and return to Japan.
8/6/1945	The United States drops the atomic bomb on Hiroshima, Japan.
8/11/1945	Japan surrenders to the Allies.
Sep, 1945	All restrictions against persons of Japanese ancestry are lifted.
1946	The International Longshoremen's and Warehousemen's Union (ILWU) organizes 28,000 sugar plantation workers to strike.
3/20/1946	Tule Lake Relocation Center is closed.
6/30/1946	The WRA closes its doors.
11/5/1946	The California Supreme Court upholds the use of the alien land law against Fred Oyama.
11/10/1946	California voters vote against a proposition that would have made the alien land law part of the state constitution.
Jul, 1947	Congress passes the Soldier Brides Act.
12/12/1947	President Harry Truman pardons all 256 Nisei who resisted the draft during the war.
1947-1951	Through a number of court cases, approximately 5,400 of the 5,700 renunciants ask that their citizenship be restored. The various court cases restore citizenships to about 5,000.
Jan, 1948	The U.S. Supreme Court rules in favor of Fred Oyama.
Jun, 1948	President Truman signs a bill into law that grants citizenship to all aliens who served in the U.S. military during World Wars I and II.

7/2/1948	President Truman signs the Japanese Evacuation Claims Act into law.
Aug, 1948	Iva Toguri is arrested and charged with eight counts of treason for her allegedly pro-Japanese activities working with Tokyo Radio during World War II.
Oct, 1948	Iva Toguri is convicted of one count of treason and sentenced to ten years in prison and a $10,000 fine. She also loses her American citizenship.
Mar, 1949	The Oregon Supreme Court declares the state's alien land laws unconstitutional.
Mar, 1950	The California Supreme Court rules that the alien land law is unconstitutional.
1952	Congress passes the McCarran-Walter Act.
Nov, 1956	California voters repeal the alien land law.
Mar, 1959	Hawaii becomes a state. Nisei veteran Daniel Inouye is elected to the U.S. House of Representatives.
1963	Inouye is elected to the U.S. Senate. Nisei veteran Spark Matsunaga is elected to replace Inouye in the House of Representatives.
1964	Hawaii is granted another seat at the House of Representatives, which is filled by Patsy Takemoto Mink.
1965	The last claim resulting from the Japanese Evacuation Claims Act is settled.
	Immigration Law abolishes national origins as a criteria for determining immigration quotas.
1967	Sansei students join other ethnic minorities in a San Francisco State University strike to demand ethnic studies programs.
1968	Sansei students join in nationwide protests against the Vietnam War and the invasion of Cambodia.
1974	Nisei war veteran George Ariyoshi is elected governor of Hawaii.
1976	Michi Weglyn publishes *Years of Infamy*.
	President Gerald Ford rescinds Executive Order 9066.
Jan, 1977	President Ford pardons Iva Toguri and restores her American citizenship.
1978	The JACL passes a resolution calling for redress for Japanese Americans interned during World War II.
1980	President Jimmy Carter signs into law the bill that creates the Commission on the Wartime Relocation and Internment of Civilians (CWRIC).
1981	The CWRIC holds nationwide hearings on the incarceration.
1982	Vincent Chin, a Chinese American, is clubbed to death in Detroit by two white men who mistake him for a Japanese.

Jan, 1983 Hirabayashi, Korematsu, and Yasui file petitions to have their wartime convictions overturned.

Feb, 1983 The CWRIC publishes *Personal Justice Denied*.

May, 1983 The National Council for Japanese American Redress (NCJAR) files a class action suit on behalf of all camp survivors against the U.S. government.

Jun, 1983 The CWRIC makes five recommendations, based on its findings.

Nov, 1983 Korematsu's wartime conviction is vacated.

Jan, 1984 Yasui's wartime conviction is vacated.

Feb, 1986 Hirabayashi's conviction for violating the evacuation order is vacated, but not his conviction for violating the curfew order.

Sep, 1987 The U.S. House of Representatives votes in favor of the five recommendations made by the CWRIC.

Jan, 1988 Hirabayashi's conviction for violating the curfew order is vacated.

Apr, 1988 The U.S. Senate votes in favor of the recommendations made by the CWRIC.

Aug, 1988 President Ronald Reagan signs into law the Civil Liberties Act of 1988.

Oct, 1988 The U.S. Supreme Court refuses to hear the NCJAR lawsuit, ending any further appeals.

Nov, 1988 President George Bush signs into law a bill that appropriates money for survivor payments.

Oct, 1990 The first payments are made to the oldest camp survivors.

May, 1992 The National Japanese American Museum opens.

11 Resources

Asian American Studies Center
University of California at Los Angeles
405 Hilgard Ave.
Los Angeles, CA 90024

Association for Multiethnic Americans
P.O. Box 191726
San Francisco, CA 94119-1726
(510) 523-2632

The AMEA was formed in November, 1988, as a national umbrella organization for twenty regional groups. Some of its local groups, such as I-Pride in Berkeley, California, were formed earlier in the 1970's. The AMEA has worked to bring the issue of multiracial identity to the attention of the public through the press. In particular, the AMEA has lobbied the U.S. Census Bureau to get a multiracial category added to forms, rather than "Other."

Japanese American Citizens League
1765 Sutter Street
San Francisco, CA 94115
(415) 921-5225

In 1930, the JACL was founded by Nisei as a civil rights organization for the Japanese American community. The JACL publishes the *Pacific Citizen*.

Japanese American Curriculum Project
234 Main Street
P.O. Box 1587
San Mateo, CA 94401
(415) 343-9408

The JACP was founded in 1970 to fight discrimination through the development of good books for use in schools' curriculum. The JACP was the first Japanese American group to tell about the concentration camp experience to schoolchildren. The JACP focuses basically on promoting the voice of Asian

Americans and is the largest distributor of Asian American books, which include *Concentration Camp USA Regulations* (1983), *Japanese American Journey* (1985), and *Wartime Hysteria: The Role of the Press* (1982).

Japanese American Library
1619 Sutter Street
San Francisco, CA 94109
P.O. Box 590598
San Francisco, CA 94159
(415) 567-5006
   In 1969, the Japanese American Library was founded as a nonprofit organization. It collects printed material on Japanese Americans in the US and Canada. The library serves as a resource for the Japanese American community, providing information on upcoming events, as well as past events. The Library is also the national repository for redress material.

National Japanese American Historical Society
1855 Folsom Street, No. 161
San Francisco, CA 94103
(415) 431-5007
   The NJAHS was founded in 1980 originally as Go for Broke, Inc. In 1981, the society created the museum exhibit "Go for Broke" about the 442nd Regimental Combat Team and the 100th Infantry Battalion. In 1982, the NJAHS published the book *Go for Broke* (1982). Its second exhibit was on the Military Intelligence Language School (MILS). In 1984, Go for Broke decided to expand its scope to include all Japanese American history. In 1985, Go for Broke changed its name officially to the National Japanese American Historical Society. Since then, it has been dedicated to preserving and promoting Japanese American history through maintaining archives and libraries, and producing traveling exhibits.

National Japanese American Museum
941 East Third Street, Suite 201
Los Angeles, CA 90013
(213) 625-0414
   The museum was founded in 1985 and opens its doors in May, 1992, to the public. The museum is the first in the United States to be dedicated solely to chronicling the Japanese American experience in the context of American history. Its first exhibit is "Issei Pioneers: Hawaii and the Mainland 1895-1924." In addition to exhibits, museum visitors can view films, attend lectures, and take part in other educational programs, all of which are intended to promote the United States' ethnic and cultural diversity.

12 Bibliography

Armor, Peter, and John Armor, with photographs by Ansel Adams and commentary by John Hersey. *Manzanar*. New York: Times Books, 1988. A winning combination of beautiful photographs by Ansel Adams and eloquent prose by John Hersey result in an excellent depiction of life at the Manzanar Relocation Center.

Chan, Sucheng. *Asian Americans: An Interpretive History*. Boston: Twayne, 1991. Chronological presentation of Japanese American history in terms of Asian Americans as a group. Helps to understand how the experiences of different Asian American groups affected each other.

Commission on Wartime Relocation and Internment of Civilians. *Personal Justice Denied*. Washington, D.C.: Government Printing Office, 1982. The report issued by the CWRIC is a good primary source for the internment and the redress movement.

Daniels, Roger. *Concentration Camps USA: Japanese Americans and World War II*. New York: Holt, Rinehart and Winston, 1972. Argues that the incarceration was not a wartime anomaly but a demonstration of deep-seated American racism compounded by hysteria.

——————————. *The Politics of Prejudice: The Anti-Japanese Movement in California and the Struggle for Japanese Exclusion*. Berkeley: University of California Press, 1962. A classic text that includes the beginning of Japanese immigration in the late 1800's to the end in 1924.

Daniels, Roger, Sandra C. Taylor, and Harry H.L. Kitano, eds. *Japanese Americans: From Relocation to Redress*. Rev. ed. Seattle: University of Washington Press, 1991. A great collection of essays, providing a broad range of perspectives and opinions on the incarceration and the redress movement. The revised edition includes a piece by Daniels on the most recent developments in the redress movement.

Fugita, Stephen S., and David J. O'Brien. *Japanese Americans: The Persistence of Community*. Seattle: University of Washington Press, 1991. In spite of their successful adaptation to American society, Japanese Americans have kept a sense of community. An interesting and complex presentation. College-level.

Houston, Jeanne Wakatsuki, and James D. Houston. *Farewell To Manzanar: A True Story of Japanese American Experience During and After the World War II Internment*. Boston: Houghton Mifflin, 1973. Jeanne Wakatsuki Houston's intensely personal account of her family's experience during and after the war.

Howe, Russell Warren. *The Hunt for "Tokyo Rose"*. Lanham, Md.: Madison Books, 1990. Describes how Iva Toguri became the victim of a witchhunt to find and punish the legendary and mythical "Tokyo Rose." Fascinating reading.

Ichioka, Yuji. *The Issei: The World of the First Generation Japanese Immigrants, 1885-1924*. New York: The Free Press, 1988. The best text on the Issei. Extremely well-written and informative.

Irons, Peter. *The Courage of Their Convictions: Sixteen Americans Who Fought Their Way to the Supreme Court*. New York: The Free Press, 1988. Gordon Hirabayashi is one of the sixteen Americans, who tells his story in his own words. Irons introduces each person, providing the historical background to their cases.

——————————. *Justice At War*. New York: Oxford University Press, 1983. Irons discovered some of the documents that resulted in erasing the wartime convictions of Gordon Hirabayashi, Fred Korematsu, and Minoru Yasui. Describes in detail the wartime cases, mostly from the point of view of the attorneys on each side.

Irons, Peter, ed. *Justice Delayed: The Record of the Japanese American Internment Cases*. Middletown, Conn.: Wesleyan University Press, 1989. A sequel to *Justice at War*, Irons describes the reopening of the three cases during the 1980's and the results. Also contains the legal documents pertaining to the three cases.

Kim, Elaine H. *Asian American Literature: An Introduction to the Writings and Their Social Context*. Philadelphia: Temple University Press, 1982. A good place to start for first-time readers of Japanese American literature. Includes a discussion of Hisaye Yamamoto.

Kitano, Harry H. L. *Japanese Americans: The Evolution of a Subculture*. Englewood Cliffs, N.J.: Prentice-Hall, Inc., 1969. A study of the community and how it has been shaped by American history and culture, particularly the role of prejudice and discrimination.

Mura, David. *Turning Japanese: Memoirs of a Sansei*. New York: Atlantic Monthly Press, 1991. As a result of a year in Japan, Mura comes to terms with his ethnic and cultural identity.

Murayama, Milton. *All I Asking for Is My Body*. San Francisco: Supa Press, 1959. In this award-winning novel, Kiyoshi Oyama grows up in pre-World War II Hawaii on a sugar plantation. Written from Kiyoshi's point of view, it is easily accessible to junior high audiences.

O'Brien, David J., and Stephen S. Fugita. *The Japanese American Experience*. Bloomington: Indiana University Press, 1991. Excellent overview of Japanese American history.

Okada, John. *No-No Boy*. Seattle: University of Washington Press, 1957. Groundbreaking novel based on the life of Hajime Jim Akutsu, who refused to answer yes to the two loyalty questions and was convicted and sentenced to prison. In the novel, the main character Ichiro tries to find a place in the post-war Japanese community after being released. Okada's depressing yet realistic depiction of a bitter, guilt-ridden community was rejected by most Japanese Americans in 1957; it was not read widely until its re-publication in 1976.

Takaki, Ronald. *Strangers from a Different Shore: A History of Asian Americans*. Boston: Little, Brown, 1989. Extremely well-written history, similar in content to Sucheng Chan's book. Has a personal tone that makes for easy reading. Includes many anecdotes.

Tateishi, John. *And Justice For All: An Oral History of the Japanese American Detention Camps*. New York: Random House, 1984. Former inmates describe camp life in their own words. Moving and often heart-wrenching history. Highly recommended.

Uchida, Yoshiko. *Desert Exile: The Uprooting of a Japanese American Family*. Autobiographical account of life in Topaz.

——————. *Journey to Topaz*. 1971.

——————. *Journey Home*. Written for junior high, these two novels fictionalize Uchida's camp and post-war experiences.

Weglyn, Michi. *Years of Infamy: The Untold Story of America's Concentration Camps*. New York: William Morrow, 1976. Considered by some to be the most important book in Japanese American history. Weglyn uncovered government documents that led to the redress movement. Appendixes include some of the documents that she and her researchers found. For high-school and college-level audiences.

Wilson, Robert A., and Bill Hosokawa. *East to America: A History of the Japanese in the United States*. New York: William Morrow, 1980. Part of the Japanese American Research Project, which was started by the JACL, this book should be read in conjunction with those by Daniels and Kitano, and the more general books by Chan and Takaki.

Yamamoto, Hisaye. *Seventeen Syllables and Other Stories*. Latham, N.Y.: Kitchen Table: Women of Color Press, 1988. Beautifully crafted stories. Provides an intimate view of Japanese American life. Can be read on many levels.

Yamauchi, Wakako. *And the Soul Shall Dance*. In *West Coast Plays* 11-12 (1982): 117-164. Award-winning play about life on a Japanese American farm during the Depression.

13 Media Materials

The Color of Honor. Loni Ding. 1987. Similar to Ding's earlier work, *Nisei Soldier* (1983), this documentary includes portraits of those who volunteered and those who refused. *The Color of Honor* was shown on public television in 1989; for many viewers, it was their first exposure to the wartime incarceration and the heroism of the 442nd and 100th.

Come See the Paradise. Directed by Alan Parker. Twentieth Century Fox, 1990. The first major film about the World War II incarceration, it has been criticized by many in the Japanese American community for its historical inaccuracies and by film critics for its poorly written script. The love story between Jack McGurn and Lily Kawamura frames the evacuation, incarceration, and return of the Kawamura family, which is broken apart by their wartime experience. Fine performances by the actor and actresses.

Days of Waiting. Directed by Steven Okazaki. Estelle Ishigo's life is movingly portrayed in this award-winning documentary. Estelle Ishigo is a Caucasian who married a Japanese American before the war and was incarcerated with him at Heart Mountain Relocation Center. The film is a heartbreaking commentary on how the evacuation and incarceration disrupted and destroyed people's lives.

Fujikawa. Directed by Mike Yoshiyuka Uno and Frank Nesbitt. Educational Film Center, 1979. This documentary provides an intimate portrait of tuna fisherman Fred Fujikawa. Fujikawa's nephew Michael Shiroishi narrates his first fishing trip with his uncle. In the course of the trip, the audience learns about Fujikawa's values and how the tuna fishing industry was pioneered by Japanese immigrants. During World War II, Fujikawa's family lost everything. After the war, he came back and built two boats with his brother, doing almost all of the work themselves.

I'm on a Mission from Buddha. Directed by Eric Hayashi. KQED TV Productions, 1992. Lane Nishikawa's one-man show was produced for public television. Nishikawa addresses many of the issues faced by the Japanese American community of the 1990's, from stereotypes to war veteran reunions to urban nightlife. Nishikawa's skits range from hilarious to poignant, but are always thought-provoking.

Nisei Soldier: Standard Bearer for an Exiled People. Directed by Loni Ding. Vox Productions, 1983. Film footage and photographs from the war front and the American concentration camps are combined with interviews with veterans of the 442nd Combat Team, 100th Infantry Battalion, and Military Intelligence Language Specialists to explain why the Nisei volunteered to fight in the war, despite the discrimination that they faced. For many, it was to prove their loyalty to the United States. Shows footage of the rescue of the Lost Battalion.

Topaz. Directed by Ken Verdoia. One West Media, 1987. What was once Utah's fifth largest city is brought to life with film footage and photographs from that time, enhanced by interviews with camp inmates and others who were involved with the evacuation and incarceration of Japanese Americans in the Topaz Relocation Center. Examines the shooting of inmate James Wakasa by a sentry guard and how the incident affected the camp. Also looks at divisive effect of the loyalty questionnaire.

Unfinished Business. Directed by Steven Okazaki. Mouchette Films, 1984. Interviews with Fred Korematsu, Minoru Yasui, and Gordon Hirabayashi are placed side by side with footage of the Sansei lawyers who volunteered to work on overturning their wartime convictions in the 1980's. The three Nisei talk about their decisions to defy the wartime evacuation and curfew orders.

DISCRIMINATION

JAPANESE AMERICANS STRUGGLE FOR EQUALITY

INDEX

Abiko, Kyutaro, 29, 31, 34, 79-80, 84
ACLU. *See* American Civil Liberties Union.
AFL. *See* American Federation of Labor.
Alien Land Laws, 32, 35, 60, 61, 87, 89, 90
All-Nisei combat team, 47, 50
American Civil Liberties Union, 47, 48
American Federation of Labor, 25, 26
Anti-Japanese movement, 27, 31, 32, 45, 94
Ariyoshi, George Ryochi, 80, 90
Asian American Studies Center, 92
Asiatic Exclusion League, 27, 86
Assembly centers, 49
Association for Multiethnic Americans, 92

Buddhism, 39, 78
Bush, George, 91

Cable Act, 87
Carter, Jimmy, 67, 83, 90
Chicago, Illinois, 59
Chin, Vincent, 76, 90
Chinese Exclusion Law, 14, 24, 39, 86
Civil Liberties Act of 1988, 69, 91

Civil Rights movement, 17, 64
Commission on Wartime Relocation and Internment of Civilians, 17, 67, 70, 71, 83, 85, 90, 94
Committee on Civil Rights, 62
Concentration camps, 41, 46, 48, 61, 92
Contract Labor, 21
Contracting, 24, 26, 79
CWRIC. *See* Commission on Wartime Relocation and Internment of Civilians.

Dekasegi, 19, 20, 29
Dekasegi-shosei, 23
DeWitt, John L., 44, 45, 71, 88, 89
Dochaku eiju, 29

Endo, Mitsuye, 48, 49, 89
Evacuation Claims Act, 62
Executive Order 589, 87
Executive Order 9066, 44, 88, 90
Executive Order 9102, 45, 88

Fair Play Committee, 54, 55
Federation of Japanese Labor, 87
Ford, Gerald, 90
442nd Regimental Combat Team, 53, 58, 59, 81, 83, 88, 93, 98
Fugita, Stephen S., 10, 94

Gentlemen's Agreement, 14, 28, 29-30, 87